COLLECTING
TOY TRAINS

Richard Friz

HOUSE OF COLLECTIBLES

NEW YORK TORONTO LONDON SYDNEY AUCKLAND

House of Collectibles and colophon are registered trademarks of Random House, Inc.

RANDOM HOUSE is a registered trademark of Random House, Inc.

This book is available at special discounts for bulk purchases for sales promotions or premiums. Special editions, including personalized covers, excerpts of existing books, and corporate imprints, can be created in large quantities for special needs. For more information, write to Special Markets/Premium Sales, 1745 Broadway, MD 6-2, New York, NY 10019 or e-mail specialmarkets@randomhouse.com.

Please address inquiries about electronic licensing of any products for use on a network, in software, or on CD-ROM to the Subsidiary Rights Department, Random House Information Group, fax 212-572-6003.

Visit the House of Collectibles Web site:
www.houseofcollectibles.com

Library of Congress Cataloging-in-Publication Data is available.

Printed in the United States of America

10 9 8 7 6 5 4 3 2 1

ISBN-13: 978-0-375-72090-1
ISBN-10: 0-375-72090-1

CONTENTS

INTRODUCTION

Toy trains, or the all-encompassing hobby of model railways, may be the oldest of America's leisure pursuits, as well as the most likely to capture the imagination of devotees of all ages. Toy train mania is truly global in scope, with manufacturers and collectors scattered across every continent. Today, train treasure troves are as likely to be unearthed in locales from Antigua to Zimbabwe as in the U.S.A.

The hobby's focus is not solely on classic locomotives and tenders, but on an endless array of rolling stock and accessories, stations, digital control systems, railside equipment and miniature engineers, flagmen, conductors, and of course, passengers. A fascinating peripheral pursuit is the paper trail that leads to train tickets, handbills, timetables, plus leading train makers' catalogs, flyers, and dealer displays.

This is an open invitation to get on track and create your own private niche of nostalgia, to operate your own private railway your way. You will begin to see these trains not as toys but a little universe in which you are the master.

All aboard!

FINDING YOUR COLLECTING GROOVE

The fascination of model railroading—the urge to build and operate a miniature railroad system—is typically American. Each individual has the opportunity to inject his own personality into his work, to create a railroad system unlike any other one in the world.—*Joshua Lionel Cowen, late Chairman of the Board, Lionel Corporation*

Part of the mystique of model railroading is that the hobby can take you over any travel route your heart desires. Many entry-level collectors find the volume and variety of what's available to be almost overwhelming.

First, don't be intimidated. When you read and hear about astronomical prices rung up for certain classic trains, keep in mind that it's the ultimate rarities that make the headlines. Only a small percentage of toy and model trains fetch industrial-strength prices, and the market is so vast that plenty of highly respectable, modestly priced train sets of considerable appeal are available. If you're stymied in finding a classic like the Baldwin 4-6-0 from the early nineteenth century or a 1928 Lionel Standard gauge Large Series Passenger Set No. 381E Bild-A-Loco or a *Hudson* 700E, keep in mind that superb replications of these and many other models may be available from a number of contemporary purveyors.

Second, be patient and exercise restraint. The biggest folly is to plunge in helter-skelter and collect every loco that suits your mojo. Not only does this spread you thin in the pocketbook, it could lead to confusion, disillusion, and burnout. There are many different types of collections to amass. Here are some examples to help you find your collecting niche.

- Be an armchair railroader and relive the fascinating history of the Iron Horse, chronicling over 200 years of real-life trains.
- Buy, or make from scratch or from model kits, realistic scale versions of any train you particularly admire, from tiny models you can hold in the palm of your hand to large live steamer riding trains you can operate outdoors.
- Develop your own sophisticated sound system and feed commands from your computer to an electronic train control system.
- Wire up your own layouts and concentrate on keeping your trains highballing it down the line.
- Specialize in models that are identified with the legendary flags of the past, such as the Baltimore & Ohio, the Erie & Lackawanna, and the Rock Island Line.
- Compile a collection based on the material from which toy trains are fashioned: vibrant lithographed paper on wood, distinctly American cast iron, delicately enameled and stenciled tinplate, realistic copper or brass.
- Document an era such as the Classic period (1923 to 1940) or Postwar (1950s to the present).
- Collect by type (for example, complete train sets vs. individual locomotives) or fill your sidings with trolley cars, cabooses, crane cars, or Pullmans.
- Collect by gauge and scale, from bold and brawny Standard and Wide gauges to the fine precision Z and N gauges.
- Collect by manufacturer or country of origin. There are diversity aplenty here and a full spectrum of gauges, colors, and price ranges.
- Or, as a purist, or hard-liner, your number one priority might be aesthetic appeal, pristine condition, and inclusion of the original box.

You may be perfectly content to admire your trains on the shelf or in display cases, or you may prefer to join the modelers who oversee the fascinating departures and arrivals of multiple sets of trains around their layouts. Modelers are heavily in the majority, with an estimated 200,000 active participants in this country alone.

This may be a simplistic observation, but whatever route you take, it is essential to collect what you like—whatever gives you the greatest satisfaction. Should the urge arise to switch to certain categories that may be in vogue at a given time, let it pass. Always buy the best example you can afford. One superb toy train is worth five lackluster models.

Do your homework. Read every book and publication on the subject you can get your hands on, consult old toy train catalogs, flyers, and price lists; research what's available on eBay. Consult Google to track down background data on train makers, museums, and collecting organizations. In this technologically advanced age, Google and other search engines are by far the most convenient means of researching your trains. Organizations such as Train Collectors of America stage shows, conduct seminars and museum tours, reprint old catalogs, and serve as conduits of information on every facet of the hobby. (See further listings under Resources.)

Above all, seek out only the most knowledgeable, reputable collectors and dealers whose integrity and judgment are impeccable. By joining the TCA you'll gain plenty of feedback from fellow members as to which dealers and auction houses have excellent track records. Those sellers who advertise in the hobby's national publications on a consistent basis also have a good reputation to uphold. Also, don't hesitate to ask the seller to furnish references of customers with whom he's done business.

There are many reasons to collect toy trains, one of which, naturally, is profit. But despite the visibility of the high-end market, starting a collection does not mean that you will wind up rich. There no denying that in recent years certain discriminating train collectors and modelers have consigned treasures to auction that reflect a remarkable appreciation in value, but that does not guarantee that it will happen to everyone. Those collectors may have been fortunate enough get in on the ground floor, having taken the plunge 20 or 30 years ago when prices weren't so crazy. There are many traits that a good collector must possess. Certainly a collector needs inner discipline, time to spare, and what Ernest Hemingway called a "built-in crap detector." It is also imperative that you have a thorough comprehension of what trains are worth, which is one of the things this book will try to teach you.

Anyone who is investment-obsessed should be well fixed financially, and be able to accept that most antiques and collectibles, by their very nature, can be volatile and cyclical. There may be days of euphoria and days when you'll experience the fiscal equivalent of a derailment. This may prove stressful and anything but relaxing. And isn't relaxation what this is all about—forgetting the cares of the world for a while, communing with fellow collectors, making new friends, and having fun? Wolfgang Richter, former managing director of the venerable German toy and train maker Ernst Paul Lehmann, once summed it up "It's a friendly hobby and a friendly business and it should stay that way."

1

WHAT TO COLLECT

Collector's Choice of Toy Train Categories

Throughout history, toy trains have been constructed using a variety of materials, from lead, tinplate, brass, wood, paper, pressed steel, and cast iron to glass, rubber, plastic, and even Bakelite. They have been powered by steam, clockwork, friction, gravity, batteries, and electricity. Trains run the gamut in size from tiny Z-, N-, and MAXI/1-scale locomotives that can fit in the palm of one's hand, to pressed-steel, pedal-powered riding trains with locomotives known to span up to six feet.

Toy trains, the oldest of the motive-powered wheeled toys in the modern era, predate toys based on other modes of land, sea, and air transport by nearly half a century. They were in the hands of children as cherished playthings in the 1830s and 1840s, almost simultaneously with the advent of the real railroads. Since the driving of the first spike of the B&O steam railway in 1828, the iron horse has stirred the imagination of young and old. Lest you think of it as a one-trick pony, railroading offers the collector many fascinating avenues of specialization to explore. Below, I will illustrate some of these.

The following are a group of terms that will appear in this chapter and throughout the book. Hopefully, by using them you will soon find yourself speaking like a pro.

- Caboose—The rear car in the lineup; often houses guards, workmen, and their equipment. British call them vans; in railroad slang: hack or shanty.
- Flags—A reference to the storied real-life railroads of the past, the B&O, NYC, etc.
- Gondola—An open freight car.
- Layout—A complete railroad system comprising locomotive, rolling stock, railside accessories.
- Locomotive—The lead unit or engine that is powered to pull the cars in tow.
- Pullman—Named for U.S. builder of sleeping cars and other rolling stock.
- Reefer—Railroad slang for a refrigerator car.
- Rolling stock—Also called consists; all the other cars that accompany the locomotive in a train set; a makeup usually associated with freight cars.
- Stock car—A car in a freight lineup hauling cattle, hogs and other livestock.
- Tanker—Or tank car, that may contain fuels, water, chemicals.
- Tender—As the name implies, this car is normally pulled directly behind the locomotive to tend to its needs with a supply of water, wood, coal, or other fuel.

Lead Toy Train Flats—1830–1850

Perhaps the earliest toy trains were simple two-dimensional lead flats cast by German tradesmen. As a by-product of the flat lead toy soldier trade, trains were similarly fashioned from molten lead and tin, poured into hollowed slate molds. Known for great period charm but without moving parts, these small primitive, affordable playthings, were sold over many years with little change in design. Train flats enjoyed a brief popularity before yielding the stage to wooden trains with moving parts, including wheels that rolled.

Wooden Trains—Early 1840s to Present

Wooden toys, the earliest mass-produced playthings, are of American and German origin. Using a combination of simple machine tools and hand-carving, toys were often fashioned by entire families as a home or cottage industry. The Tower Guild of Massachusetts, Charles Crandall of Pennsylvania, and Ellis, Britton, and Eaton of Vermont were the best known wooden toy makers on these shores. The major output of wooden trains in Germany came from the Erzgebirge and Sonneberg forest regions. Carvers here were overseen by a handful of wholesale firms who produced the catalogs and handled distribution. The first wooden toy train entries were crude and unadorned but, unlike tinplate and cast iron, were childproof and durable. Later, wooden trains became more elaborate, with the addition of hand painting and stenciling.

Since the 1880s, the wooden trains of choice were linear double-sided examples embellished with fanciful, brightly colored lithographic paper glued to the wood surface. This transformation allowed for far greater attention to detail, even so far as depicting passengers in their coaches and the engineer waving from his cab. Some versions included a detachable standing brakeman.

Lithographed wooden train makers that resonate with collectors include Massachusetts purveyors Milton Bradley, Morton E. Converse, McGloughlin Brothers, Whitney S. Reed, Gibbs Mfg. Co. of Ohio, and Rufus Bliss, Rhode Island. Most of the above makers' catalogs also offered a wide range of doll furniture, spinning tops, target games, pasteboard train jigsaw puzzles, board games, and building blocks. Blocks were often included as a bonus with train sets, serving as cargo on flatcars or coaches.

Toward the turn of the century, toy trains had so captured youngsters' fancies that Milton Bradley, Bliss, and others obliged with sets in greater variety, and in

Morton Converse train station with passenger train set, 1890s.

R. Bliss Golden Gate Special lithograph paper-on-wood set, with *Gen. Grant* locomotive, 1880s: $7,150— Bertoia's Kuehnle Sale 2005.

a choice of sizes. No finer large-scale examples exist than an 1891 five-piece Bliss Chicago Limited set that measures 48 inches long or a Milton Bradley Flyer set with *Hercules* locomotive spanning 45 inches. Often sets were offered in several sizes. The popular Bliss Barnum Circus Train, for example, featured cage wagons in 19 inches and 28 inches. Comic toy collectors were especially attracted by sets such as the Bliss Brownie Picnic, which featured a locomotive and two gondola cars carrying 21 cut-out Palmer Cox Brownie figures.

New York maker Fisher-Price, from 1931 to the early 1960s, put a whole new spin on lithographed paper-on-wood toys. Fisher-Price produced a line of whimsical pull toys for the toddler set that often included bellows, bells, chimes, whistles, and other sound effects. Another purveyor, Gibbs Mfg. of Ohio, continues to produce lithographed wooden tops and toys to this day. The hobby has seen a recent resurgence in simple, unpainted, rather spartan wooden train sets, notably by small New England woodworking firms.

Tinplate Clockwork and Push-Pull Toy Trains—1830s–Early 1900s

Early tinplate toy train entries tended to be fragile, fantasy creations, erratic in motion, with out-of-proportion smokestacks, exaggerated cabs, and oversized bells. Wood, tinplate, and later cast-iron trains first evolved as carpet runners or floor trains. Without benefit of track or power source, it was up to youngsters to provide the train's *push-pull* direction of movement. Most often, American units consisted only of a locomotive with tender, in a manageable size of six to eight inches. Toward the late 1860s, child-power free-runners gave way to a sturdy machined brass or steel spring-wound clockwork drive system with interlocking gears that when key-wound, propelled the train into an erratic 30-minute run as the spring uncoiled. By the late 1890s, the windup mechanism was housed in sturdier cast-iron frames. These well-machined clockwork mechanisms are not to be confused with the later so-called *windups* whose cheaper tinplate gears actually died down within two or three minutes.

Inertial flywheel-powered trains were popular from 1900 to 1930. The first examples, introduced in the 1880s, created motion by fastening a string wound to the flywheel; when pulled, it sent the flywheel spinning. Later, a cast-iron (Europeans often used lead) central inertia wheel or flywheel serves to drive the spring-powered toy that surges forward as motion is transmitted by the locomotive's rear wheels (i.e., power wheels). Although some toys rely on an auxiliary spring lever starting device, most are activated by rubbing the locomotive across the floor a few times to spin the flywheel, creating friction, and then letting go. This rather awkward procedure loses precious seconds, especially if the engine is to be coupled to the cars, so running time is necessarily brief.

The first manufacturer to produce tin trains with *clockwork mechanisms* was George W. Brown & Company of Forrestville, Connecticut, beginning in 1856. Leading toy authority Jack Herbert once observed that Brown's designer must have a had a wee nip of the sauce before sitting down at his drafting board to create the Red Bird, "as everything appears enchantingly out of proportion."

Brown was soon joined by other established clockmaking Connecticut firms who added trains to their line of clocks as a profitable sideline, such as Ives-Blakeslee, Union Manufacturing (later acquired by Hull & Stafford), and Merriam Manufacturing. Pennsylvania innovators included James Fallows and Fallows' parent firm, Francis, Field & Francis of Philadelphia. Another early maker, Althof Bergmann of New York City, also wore the hat of dealer/distributor.

Locomotives and cars were stamped out from sheets of tinned iron or steel, then painted or japanned tinplate. (Japanning is a decorative process using a coat of lacquer added to several layers of paint, for a durable, glossy finish.) Catchy names (e.g., Victory, Boss, Nero, *Flash,* Pegasus, and Excelsior) or call letters of leading railroads, such as B&O and NYC, were boldly stenciled in black or gilt on the chassis of engines, tenders, and cars. The most popular locomotives featured two large driving wheels under the cab, with two smaller wheels forward and on the frame beneath the smokestack. Wheels were highly decorative and thin, but often of sturdy cast iron and embellished with delightful arabesques of hearts and other geometric patterns. Top-of-the-line locomotives invariably were colored in bright red and gold. Cabs and boilers were embellished with flowers, laurels, and other delicate flourishes to enliven an otherwise basic design. The *cowcatcher,* another typically American toy train feature, is a plow-shaped projection fronting the locomotive, which serves to clear the

Ernst Plank
Locomotive,
1882.

tracks ahead of snow, debris, and presumably, curious cattle.

Locomotive sizes were all over the spectrum, ranging from a tiny eight-inch Fallows Dexter to the aptly named Ives Giant, at 33 inches arguably the largest and most desirable U.S. tin toy train ever made. A delightful feature of the Stevens & Brown Pegasus is a figure of the engineer whose hand connects to a wire that rings a bell activated as the wheels turn. An 1880s Ives catalogue tells us that its Whistler locomotive makes boys very happy. With a patented whistle attachment, it came in 12½- and 15-inch sizes.

Track was still unheard of, as were train stations, bridges, tunnels, and other rail-side accessories, leaving it up to imaginative youngsters to improvise using shoeboxes, cardboard tubing, and other makeshift materials. Remarkably, during the three decades (1860–1890) that marked the heyday of American tin trains, manufacturers showed little design creativity, as locomotives from the 1890s were near-clones of those produced 30 years earlier.

A handful of small German companies, the earliest being Mathias Hess in 1826, created trackless push-pull tinplate trains for the European as well as the American market. These trains tended to be elaborate constructions for the wealthy. Pioneer German makers were clustered mostly in the Nuremberg sector, in proximity to the tin mines. Small firms, mostly family owned, included Karl Bub, Lutz, Ernst Plank, Rock & Graner, Issmayer, Gottfried Striebel, and Buchner, who were joined in 1859 by Gebrüder Märklin. In the early 1900s, Nuremberg-style tinplate trains by the above German makers were known for detailed solder construction and hand painted and varnished finishes.

Gebrüder Märklin, originally known for miniature pots and pans and doll house accessories, was destined to become known as the preeminent toy train maker of the ages—the sole survivor of the above elite group, and still active on the toy train scene today. Lehmann, another old-line maker, opened its doors in 1881 with both key-wind and friction tinplate toys. Joining the list of German makers who soon outgrew the domestic market and expanded their vistas to Great Britain, France, and the U.S. were Gebrüder Bing, Gunthermann, Carette, Fleishmann, Falk & Doll, and Distler.

Among most the visible French makers, many better known by their initials, were Emile Favre, Georges Parent, Jouets en Paris (J.E.P.), Radiguet & Massiot, J. Caron, and Charles Rossignol of Paris. Rossignol, in particular, was a master at ignoring scale, adorning superstructures and coaches with lithography so realistic as to simulate grit and grime splashed on the locomotive. French tinplate entries were of thin sheet tin, usually embossed for added strength. Cheaper entries were spirit-painted (a mixture of resin and volatile oil) and colors were known to fade when exposed to UV rays. French tinplate trains rolled on spidery, frail spoke wheels of lead; oversized chimneys gave them a top-heavy appearance. The Gallic preference was for complete train sets (or liveries) comprising as many as five cars closely resembling our American stage coaches. A very small, six-inch-long Favre locomotive, ca. 1865, pulling tender and three cars featured a simulated wooden boiler and a powerful clockwork mechanism. Much larger specimens still displayed marvelous delicacy.

The following highly specialized or toy train categories were produced in a multitude of incarnations and materials.

Penny Toys: 1890–1935

Fifty years ago, the late toy authority Leslie Daiken, in the Illustrated *London News,* entitled his article, "Only one penny—and all one penny: Penny toys—the delight of children in the past and a lasting record of changing fashions." London street vendors in late Victorian England were one of the principle outlets for penny toys. They were also found in regular toy stores as toys, Christmas tree decorations, candy containers, stocking stuffers, or in tiny boxes as party favors. Penny toys, a minuscule two to four inches long, can be held in the palm of one's hand.

Most collectors think of rather fragile penny toys as being made exclusively of painted, stained, or lithographed tinplate. In fact, the most fervently pursued tinplate comprises less than 25 percent of the penny objects sold. Such diverse materials were used as cast iron, wood, lead, celluloid, zinc cast, and even paper. Certain examples were also made from natural materials; e.g., a dried walnut shell containing a fold-out sheet of miniature photographs, titled "London in a Nutshell."

Most penny toys were made in and around Nuremberg and exported to Great Britain and the U.S. German makers cleverly tailored toys to specific markets, so one is likely to find London omnibuses and ambulances, French postal vans, and American motorcycles and locomotives, all made by German firms. The

German Hess penny toy train set, boxed, 1920s.

German, possibly Meier, locomotive, penny toy, 1920s.

earliest known locomotive example, a four-inch friction driven penny toy by an unknown German maker, dates back to 1900. The most prolific manufacturer of penny toys by far was Johann Philipp Meier although other German firms such as Distler, Einfalt, Fischer, Hess, Issmayer, and Kellerman are also well represented. French manufacturers include Fauve, Jouets en Paris, Saint Mihiel, Jeune, Simon, and Rossignol; in Spain there was Paya, and in Japan, Toyodo and C.K. (a firm known only by its trademark intials).

Inexpensive, whimsical and amusing, these paltry geegaws brought playthings within the reach of even the poorest families. Today penny toys find appeal from crossover doll house collectors and miniaturists, as well as toy enthusiasts, and the more scarce entries are known to bring prices well up into five figures—anything but penny ante.

Live Steam Trains: 1880s–Early 1900s
The British led the way with toy locomotives propelled by steam and constructed of solid brass. Though made as early as the mid-1840s, steam trains were technically advanced, and were priced well beyond the allowances of young lads. Usually cabless, early live steam trains were rather spartan affairs and bore no more than a spectacle plate (to protect the engineer from the elements, this vertical metal projection featured a pair of round windows resembling spectacles, hence the term). Locomotives featured a firebox, kerosene or alcohol lamp, a boiler, and a steam chest to store power. A pulley system or similar apparatus was integral to the power system that drove the wheels. While potentially explosive and best left in the hands of adults, the operation of toy steam trains almost exactly duplicated that of full-size steam trains. Realism was the greatest draw of these toy steamers.

Typically, nascent designs were patterned after the earliest trains and were successfully produced for decades without change. They were easily identified by their large boilers, towering out-of-proportion stacks and assorted valves, and oversized pistons. As a touch of British irony, these trains, despite being endowed with exotic names—Britannia, Invicta, Empress Queen, Zulu, and Thunderer—were referred to indelicately as "dribblers" or "piddlers," so named for their tendency to leave a puddle or water trail due to condensation deposited by steam cylinders. Leading British firms included Stevens Model Dockyard, Clyde Model Dockyard, Whitney's, J. Bateman & Co., H.J. Wood, Newton & Co., Bowman Co., and Wallwork.

Many British makers stuck with steamers up though the 1920s, but seemed reluctant to offer anything but the rather prosaic models of early prototypes that had been operating for 40 or 50 years. Rarely did an engine include a tender. A notable exception, a ca. 1890 Newton 2-2-2 (an engine wheel configuration

Carette I-gauge live steam locomotive, 1897.

of two pilots, two drivers and two trailers) featured gleaming brass with a special plate engraved with Newton's name and London Fleet Street address. It spanned nine inches with tender.

Steam trains were taken more seriously as scientific toys as opposed to frivolous playthings for youngsters. Stevens, which is known to have marketed at least 18 different designs of this type of toy train, featured steamers in their catalogues as late as 1926. The French firm Radiguet & Massiot produced a diverse range of rather archaic designs, and remained the most respected manufacturer of model steam locomotives until the end of the nineteenth century.

Early U.S. steam train makers included Buckman, Weeden, and Eugene Beggs. Ives also produced steam outline trains which appear to be steam-propelled, but may actually run by electricity or clock-work, and still retained a Wide-gauge steam set in its line into the 1920s. Despite being a nation engaged in building the world's foremost steam railway network, toy steamers in America never achieved the popularity they enjoyed in Europe.

For nearly 30 years, until the end of the century, steam sets made by Eugene Beggs and later Jehu Garlick typified the best American toy trains. As early as 1872, Beggs introduced a smart, well-designed toy steam locomotive modeled on the American outline (large headlamp, tall smokestack, a bell, and no splashers or mud guards). Beggs also innovated with strip rails so the locomotive could travel in circles. The Beggs steamers had one drawback—price. Not everyone could afford paying up to $30 a set when a dollar a day was considered a living wage.

Stevens Model Dockyard, Wide-gauge steam locomotive, early 1900.

Many collectors save their superlatives for the beautifully proportioned little seven-inch Weeden Dart, introduced in 1888 to the low-end market to close the gap between the expensive Beggs trains. The Dart set included a light-gauge tin coach and tender and sold with a circle of track in the $3 range. It proved an instant success, selling in the tens of thousands, and its popularity lasted well into twentieth century.

Pioneer German steam train specialists Jean Schonner and Ernst Plank were soon joined by Gebrüder Märklin and Bing, Rock & Graner, Georg Fischer, Georges Carette, Peter Doll et Cie, Issmayer, and Lutz (which was later acquired by Märklin).

The marquee entry among European live steamers, Märklin's gauge 1 *Stephenson's Rocket,* was introduced in 1910. It marked the firm's first foray into historical trains with a faithful replica of legendary real-life British speedster that left competition in the dust in the Rainhill racing trials. The first powered passenger train, the *Rocket,* combined many new features and proved a major leap forward in locomotive design. With its high stack, it measured nine inches tall and was eight inches long.

The hobby has seen a resurgence in live steam toy trains and several contemporary firms are issuing renditions of early classics. Crossover collecting interest, including those whose focus is on scientific and educational steam toys, particularly from Great Britain and Germany, make for a highly competitive market.

Cast-iron Toy Trains: 1880–1930s

Cast-iron trains are almost exclusively an American phenomenon, the exception being Wallwork, an English foundry, which produced a handful of trains in this material in the early 1890s. Cast-iron examples cornered the toy train market by the late nineteenth century. With the possible exclusion of Ives and Hubley, which produced a number of unwieldy key-wind engines in cast-iron, most trains and train sets in this medium were usually trackless and relied on child power.

Though ruggedly built, cast-iron locomotives were a handful to move around, especially for toddlers. Due to its brittle makeup, cast iron also is susceptible to chipping and cracking.

Coupling of locomotives with cars was literally a snap, relying on hook-and-eye or cast pin-to-hole mechanisms. Sizes varied all over the spectrum. A Hubley steam profile engine and a Jerome Secor Puck were both only six inches long; a husky Carpenter "870" locomotive and tender (shared with Secor as being the first patented cast-iron train, in June 1880) spanned 21½ inches. Ives claimed their 1893 *Cannonball Express* floor train (engine, tender, and two cars) to be the largest cast-iron train set made, at 55-inches overall. Pratt & Letchworth could very well dispute that claim with its "880" *Buffalo Express* from 1891, modeled after the record-holding prototype which averaged 112.5 miles per hour. With a tender and two coaches it spanned five feet.

Brawny cast-iron versions were admired for their detailing, authenticity, and ability to capture the essence of the genuine article. Early pioneers in cast-iron trains included Ives-Blakeslee and Francis W. Carpenter. They were soon joined by Wilkins Toy Company, Hubley, Dent Hardware, Kenton Hardware, J.&E. Stevens (also the most prolific and renowned purveyor of mechanical banks), and Harris Toy Company. A number of leading makers, including Pratt &

Ives Anderson clockwork locomotive, pat. 1884.

Carpenter Canadian Pacific No. 187, 1890.

Letchworth, also produced metal parts for the real life railroad industry.

For over half a century, cast-iron toy trains ruled as a truly American art form. Because of the scarcity of classic examples that have survived intact, with good paint, shady practitioners have reproduced them to a fare-thee-well. Although relatively easy to detect, repros have made collectors gun-shy, which may account for the cyclical nature of the market for cast-iron toy trains.

Pressed-Steel Trains: Early 1900s to Present

Often oversized, more stylized than detailed, brawny pressed-steel trains that could actually support a man's weight had the aura of being indestructible.

Because of the weight factor, most examples were of the push-pull, gravity-propelled type, or, in the case of the oversize riding or pedal cars, relied on a child's pedal power. Early pressed-steel giants included Kingsbury Toy Co., Buddy "L", D.P. Clark, Keystone Mfg., Metalcraft, Structo Mfg., and pedal train makers American National, Corcoran Mfg., Kelmet, Garton Toy Co. (noted for its 1961 Casey Jones Cannonball Express Locomotive), Steelcraft (renamed the Murray-Ohio Products Co. after World War II), and Gendron Wheel Co. (Pioneer Line). In Great Britain, Triang and Lines Brothers produced pedal locomotives.

David P. Clark, renamed the Schieble Toy and Novelty Company in 1909, produced a wide range of rugged wood and pressed-steel friction toys in their Hill Climber line, including handsome locomotives and trolleys. Most pedal locomotives measured at least three feet with an average size of 45 inches. Oversized pressed-steel vehicles, measuring 12 to 30 inches long, were usually of the push-pull type, although Kingsbury used a powerful sealed clockwork motor as its drive mechanism.

The odds-on favorite pressed-steel oversized outdoor train set is the early 1930s Buddy "L" beauty consisting of clockwork locomotive, tender, tank car, and caboose, with other specialty cars and even a roundhouse also available. The big knock on pedal cars is that they usually show signs of having taken such a beating from youngsters over the years that they appear to be relics from a roller derby. Few have survived in pristine condition and retained their original paint. Regrettably, in the case of most entries offered at auction today the operative word is "restored," which greatly detracts from value. It's a scenario of too many hardcore collectors vying for a dwindling number of rider toys that were produced in limited quantities in the first place.

Electric Trains: 1884 to Present
Most toy train faithful consider electric trains (excluding scratch-builts and scale models fashioned from

kits—another ballgame entirely) to be the "little engine that could," the driving force of the hobby. Electric train prices tend to be less prone to cyclical glitches than trains of tin, lithographed wood, cast iron, or other materials. One seldom sees dramatic upswings or prices bottoming out on electric trains at auctions or shows. Though considered failures when first introduced, such classic flops as the 1929 Ives' Prosperity Special (bad timing—it was the eve of Depression) and 1957 Lionel's Lady Lionel (misguided, as little girls apparently wanted trains like their brothers had and *not* in pastel colors) have since found redemption. Short-lived production runs insure scarcity and trigger a stratospheric asking price in today's market. Along with mechanical banks and Liberty dollars, classic electric toy trains appear to be recession-proof. On the other hand, more post–World War II model electric trains command four- and five-figure prices today than any other contemporary toy genre; only a handful of 1950s robots and space toys have escalated so much in value over such a brief span of time.

Carlisle & Finch brought out an electric tram in 1897, claiming to be the first successful U.S. maker of electric trains. In reality, the earliest electric train on record was a unit on raised tracks that operated on two dry-cell batteries. Called the Elevated Railway, it is illustrated in an 1892 Horsman catalog. Presumably,

it evolved from a patent granted to a Murray Bacon and assigned to Novelty Electric Co. of Philadelphia in 1884.

Electric trains did not gain universal appeal at first; in the U.S., although there were some earlier inroads, electrically powered toy trains were not widely available until 1910.

Carlisle & Finch, of Cincinnati, opened for business in 1896 with a three-rail direct-current trolley. Other pioneers, often hailed as the "gauge II aristocracy" included Howard Company, Knapp Electric & Novelty Company, and Voltcamp Electric; Lionel, the preeminent name in U.S. trains and today's sole "Big Four" survivor (American Flyer, Ives, and Marx being the other three) entered the fray in 1901 with an ungainly battery-powered flat car in 2⅞ inch gauge. Ives, Blakeslee, which had a heavy early commitment to clockwork trains, and in fact continued to market them over the next 15 years, delayed their first electric entry, patterned after a New York Central protoype, until 1910. Ives adopted O gauge as their standard, producing almost identical copies of popular Märklin and Issmayer European I-gauge trains. In 1907, American Flyer introduced locomotives in cast iron that were literally clones of the Ives cast-iron steam outline 0-4-0, but with a lower price tag. It was not until 1918, however, that American Flyer made the plunge with their first electric train, the Model 1225 Type 1 Hummer O gauge. Dorfan, a latecomer, introduced their first electric model, the Electric Constructive Locomotive, in 1925.

German-made electric trains were again led by Märklin, as by 1902 they offered a complete line of electric-drive, steam-outline locomotives and train

Lady Lionel train set in pastel colors, 1957.

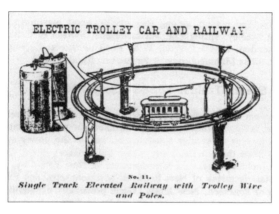

ELECTRIC TROLLEY CAR AND RAILWAY

No. 11.
Single Track Elevated Railway with Trolley Wire and Poles.

Novelty Electric Elevated Railway No. 11, probably the first U.S. electric train, patented in 1884; appeared in 1892 Horsman catalog.

sets. Bing, meanwhile, delayed production of electric trains in any quantity until 1908 or 1909. Carette, which made an early incursion with a tram in 1892, added a gauge-III Stirling Single Deluxe engine made for the British market in 1902, but struggled with quality and reliability problems. By the early twentieth century, several noted German firms had folded after failing to meet the challenge of electric powered trains. The venerable firm founded by Ernst Paul Lehmann that had turned out clockwork and string-wind-driven tin belatedly entered the electric train field in 1968. Under the name Lehmann Gross Bahn (LGB), the firm continues to this day to produce oversized G-scale electric trains on a worldwide basis.

At first, the British were skittish about electric power. In 1906 their two leaders in the field, Bassett-Locke and Gamages, listed over 300 models of locomotives, yet only one, a Märklin 2-4-0 Charles Dickens, was electric. By this time, the Germans clearly reigned supreme in the British toy train market. Firms such as Bassett-Locke, while creating the aura of manufacturing their own trains, relied almost completely on German imports. Hornby, one of the few local makers, trumpeted their Meccano Ltd. line, while only a handful of London brass "dribblers" remained and struggled to gain market share. On the high end, Märklin and Bing churned out oversize, expensive gauge-I locomotives for London's A.W. Gamage and W. Bassett-Locke, who acted as retailers and distributors. Less expensive sets made by Gebrüder Bing, Georges Carette, Karl Bub, Kraus, H. Fischer, and J. Fleischmann were channeled through British toy emporiums and large department stores.

Novelty Comic and Circus Trains:
1920s to Present

This is a diverting spin-off that is more apt to attract cross-collectors of comic and circus toys than modelers and toy train purists, who are prone to agonize at the very sight of these novelty items. Most novelty trains are based on pure whimsy, with little attention to scale and realism, as personified by the 1936 Marx Animal Express figural bunny locomotive with thrashing hind legs. The popular Disney handcar versions usually are a combination of cast steel and tinplate, with composition figures with arms and legs of hard rubber. Most examples are animated by rugged key-wind motors, although later versions tend to be battery operated.

Disney and other comic-inspired handcars featuring Mickey and Minnie Mouse, Peter Rabbit, Popeye and Olive Oyl, Donald Duck and Pluto, Moon Mullins and Kayo, and Fred and Barney from the Flintstones are vigorously pursued by collectors. Highly coveted circus train sets often come complete with scenic backgrounds and tents, clowns and other big-top performers, and caged animals. Some examples of these include the Ives 1930s Wide-gauge circus set, the Wells & Company, Ltd., and Lionel Mickey Mouse circus trains from the 1930s, and the record-breaking Märklin Oriental circus train from the early 1900s. All write their own ticket at auction.

The following toy train spin-offs, often referred to as collaterals or peripherals, further reflect the scope and diversity of the hobby.

Railroadiana: 1850s to Present

Railroadiana, which refers to anything that relates to toy trains and railroads, exclusive of the train or railroad itself, is attracting a growing number of collectors. Since this is such a broad category, prices for these items vary widely. In the scheme of collecting values they run the gamut from passenger ticket stubs, normally worth mere pocket change, to a beautifully cast bell, ca. 1920, from a New Haven Railroad locomotive 0107, that might bring a small fortune. This category's spectrum of pursuits, among which toy trains are merely a footnote, embraces several distinct types: ephemera (paper disposables) and hardware (often referred to as three-dimensional items). A further breakout of artifacts relates to the actual railways: brass whistles, bells, oilcans, uniforms, caps and other regalia, lanterns, locks, keys, headlights, railroad watches, silverware, and china and other dining car place settings. Many of these items can be distinguished by the insignia of a particular flag or rail line.

Another type of ephemera relates to the profusion of promotional material issued by toy manufacturers themselves, such as catalogs, flyers, decals, cap and jacket patches, posters, in-store displays, calendars, and booklets and guides supplying plans and sketches for building various train layouts. Then there's the paper trail left by real-life train lines of yesteryear, recalling such long defunct railway legends (known as "fallen flags") as Super Chief, City of Portland, Twentieth Century Limited, Burlington Zephyr, Atchison, Topeka and Santa Fe, Wabash Cannonball, and York & Peachbottom. Probably the most readily available and affordable rail-line ephemera is the proliferation of paper or pasteboard railroad

Lionel Mickey Mouse Circus Train Set, Wald Disney Enterprises, early 1930s: $6,050— Bertoia's Kuehnle Sale, 2005.

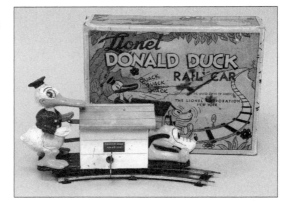

Lionel Donald Duck & Pluto handcar, 1940: $1,045— Bertoia's Kuehnle Sale, 2005.

timetables. Early specimens are stark, simply printed sheets; later, stock woodcut illustrations of steam trains appeared on everything from handbills, to posters, tickets, and timetables. Beginning in the early twentieth century, vibrant, lavish art-deco and art-nouveau illustrations of posh dining cars and surging locomotives promoted the romance of rail travel.

Early timetables often featured enlightening footnotes and advisories. Dave Peters Sr., in a railroadiana feature in the *Time-Life Encyclopedia of Collectibles*, cites a listing from the 1880s which was exasperatingly noncommittal about the actual time of arrival, stating only: "Passengers will be conveyed as quickly as possible to the end of the line." In 1877, with all the confusion over differences in various time zones and each city on the line setting their own clock by the sun, a Pennsylvania Railroad timetable alerted passengers as follows: "Standard Time from NYC to Pittsburgh is Philadelphia local time, which is five minutes behind New York time and runs 19 minutes ahead of Pittsburgh time." Trainmen's rules-of-operation manuals also offer intriguing insights. A 1908 Erie Railroad manual even spelled out the laws in various states as to when and where a passenger and his baggage could be ejected for failure to pay his fare (Hopefully, not in the middle of the Mojave Desert).

Who would have thought that a collection of railroad passes would roll to record heights at auction? Annual passes were freely handed out to politicians, favored business tycoons, and railroad personnel. Recently, a collection of nearly a thousand passes was sold by Philip Weiss Auctions from a consignor whose grandfather, H.M. Bronson, the original owner, received a free ride on the rails as a railway employee from 1865 to 1905. The passes featured tiny vignettes and bore banners of long-defunct lines as the Richmond & Danville Railroad Company (dated 1885) and the Ashville & Chattanooga Railroad (1868). Broken down in smaller lots, averaging $2,000 per lot, collectors doled out a total of $70,000.

Also fairly common, railroad company stock certificates are usually punched with cancellation holes, denoting that the stock has been redeemed or that the firm has ceased operation. A sizeable, highly specialized group of collectors pursue these certificates, which are often embellished with colorful lithography. Shares in leading train makers, American Flyer and Lionel common stock in particular, are true works of art, embellished with vibrant illustrations. A rule of thumb, applicable to all types of railway ephemera, is that collectors place a higher premium on certificates issued by a line that proved a financial bust or ran on short routes in relative obscurity. Such items often sell at a premium.

Other paper categories pursued by crossover specialists include postcards of noted flagship trains and trading cards. Lionel issued a set of cards in the post–World War II years that depicted classics such as the M.K.T. Texas Special diesel, the Union Pacific Diesel Switcher, and Great Northern Electric embellished with logos of these flag lines.

Railroad diner menu collectors could no doubt recite the old "Chattanooga Choo-Choo" refrain, "Dinner in the diner, nothing could be finer than to have your ham and eggs in Carolina." A fascinating 1920s Northern Pacific Railroad diner menu features far more lavish breakfast fare, including champagne, shirred eggs, broiled tenderloin steak, fried oysters on toast, and other delicacies, all for one dollar for adults.

In our experience, most of the more memorable private toy train collections tie in highly displayable, graphically appealing railroadiana with their track layouts to follow a unifying concept or theme—one that conveys not only convincing realism, but a feeling of nostalgia for a certain time and place. This category can be defined as being comprised of hardware or relics from real-life railways of yore. Signal lamps or lanterns are always favorites with collectors, especially when clearly identified by a flagship line. At Noel Barrett's May 2005 sale of the Ward Kimball train collection, an example of a plain glass etched Santa Fe lamp, paired with a lamp in ruby glass marked "V. &T.R.R.," both 16 inches high, sold as one lot at $9,900 (vs. a $100–200 pre-sale estimate). Most conductor's lamps have an unusually long bail or handle, allowing it to be swung freely in a wide arc to signal the engineer.

Train whistles came into use in Great Britain as early as 1833, and solid brass or chrome engine whistles are like sculpted works of art. A highly decorative foot-high example from the 1870s is powered by compressed air and can sound three notes. (It is reminiscent of the whistle legendary folk hero Casey Jones made to "sing like a whippoorwill" along the Salt Lake Line.)

Highly collectible, these early menus conjure up exotic diner fare on the Northern Pacific and New York Central lines.

Builder's plates of brass or chrome identify in embossed lettering the maker of the engine, and indicate class, voltage, place and date of manufacture, and in some cases technical specifications. Extremely scarce, they're high on collectors' want lists of railway hardware.

Railway company depot or ticket office signs in reverse lithography on glass, embossed tin, or heavy cardboard, and full-color lithographed railroad company calendars have a special cachet with ephemera collectors.

Brass and steel locks and keys which secured switches, signals, coaches, freight cars, tool boxes, equipment sheds, and ticket offices; the most desirable bear the imprint of the line itself, the earlier and more obscure the better.

Cast-iron switch stands with signal lamps, semaphores, and R.R. crossing stands are admired by collectors of decorative curiosities, folk art, and by interior decorators as well as railroadiana diehards. Rail spikes were commonly used between 1912 and 1931 and phased out by most railway lines by 1940. Spikes (or date nails), commonly embossed with numbers on their heads, were embedded in railroad ties to record the date a rail section was repaired or replaced.

Selection of real-life railroad hardware and ephemera, Barrett's Kimball Sale I, 2004.

Rubber stamps and ticket punches in unusual shapes and sizes were used in ticket offices or by ticket takers for well over half a century from 1890 to 1950. Punches were specially tooled to make identifiable holes in the ticket (e.g., "baggage checked" or the numerals 1 and 2 for half-fare tickets).

Brass or chrome curved hat plates or badges were attached to hats of the on-train personnel that identified their duties (e.g., conductor, trainman, ticket collector, brakeman, porter). Brass uniform buttons embossed with the names of the nation's most venerable flagship lines are often prominently framed or displayed in shadow boxes.

Brass or chrome luggage/mail bag tags, notched for leather strap holders, were stamped with numbers bearing the name of the railway painted black or gold. An arresting array of a half-dozen tags etched with names of old-line railways, including Wiscasset (Maine) RR and Quebec, and V&T (Virginia & Truckee), sold briskly at $3,025 at Barrett's Kimball Sale II in May 2005.

Tin or brass kerosene torches and oil cans for lubricating valves on steam locomotives date from the 1930s and 1940s. Especially desirable are engraved brass oilcans presented to noted dignitaries or to railroad employees honored for performing beyond the call of duty, or for years of faithful service.

Toy Train Consumer Catalogs

Since train collecting relies so extensively on correctly identifying engines, rolling stock, and accessories by manufacturer's number, letter designations, and photographs, dealer catalogues constitute the hobby's single most viable and ardently pursued ephemeral offshoot. Not only are these catalogs, which Lionel called "wish books," indispensable as references, they're a visual treat as well, and chronicle dramatic styling changes in train sets and peripherals, gauge preference, and choice of motive power.

Numerous vintage Ives, Gamage, Bassett-Locke, Hornby, Märklin, and Lionel catalogs have been reproduced, most notably by such collecting organizations as the Toy Train Operating Society and Train Collectors Association (TCA), as well as a two-volume set from Greenberg Publishing featuring catalogs dating from 1923 to 1942.

The originals, however, are the only ones of intrinsic value, and certain scarce examples by Elektoy, Ives, and American Flyer have been known to exact prices at auction nearly as steep as the train sets depicted. Marx, American Flyer, and Lionel also issued train sets marketed exclusively through department stores, and that never appeared in their own catalogs. Those catalogs were circulated by Sears Roebuck (e.g., the All State sets), Macy's, Montgomery Ward , J.C. Penney, and other mercantile giants from the 1920s and 1930s, and rate high with collectors.

In 1909 Ives, Blakeslee, following the lead of German and English makers, introduced a catalog with the then-revolutionary concept of targeting its message to an imaginary 12-year-old boy, as opposed to a

Railroad signal lantern; Canadian Pacific brass railroad car lock and key; locomotive bell; Pennsylvania Railroad metal plaque—Maurer's Ritter Sale, 2005.

Ives Train Catalogs, 1920s.

American Flyer Catalogs, 1928, 1930s.

wholesaler or retail distributor. Though a bit cornball, this personal touch helped build a cult of Ives loyalists that exists even today.

Ironically, in 1930, even with Ives in bankruptcy and in the process of a takeover by Lionel and American Flyer, the Bridgeport maker produced what many consider its most stunning catalog—an art-deco set-

ting of Ives headliners streaming forth from a brilliant white metropolitan terminal.

Lionel's first known catalog in 1902 featured a line drawing of the City Hall Trolley. Cowen went to a full-color catalog in 1910.

The catalog of American Flyer's predecessor Edmonds-Metzel Mfg. (1907–1909) illustrated 11 clockwork trains, all passenger sets. The first catalog to be identified by the trade name American Flyer appeared in 1910.

Another sought-after catalog, a 1948 A.C. Gilbert-American Flyer pocket-sized edition, features Superman on its cover swooping up, up, and away for a visit to the Gilbert Hall of Science in NYC.

In 1923, for the first time, a father and son were pictured on the Lionel catalog cover. The young lad, labeled as "The Happy Lionel Boy" in catalogs and other promotional literature, was none other than Joshua Cowen's son Lawrence. Lionel's enduring marketing ploy of father and son bonding while running their trains was soon imitated ad nauseum by rival train makers. Attesting to the realism of Lionel trains, a 1931 catalog featuring Bob Butterfield, a Twentieth Century Railroad engineer, was captioned, "The Train that Railroad Men Buy for Their Boys." As a tie-in to the catalog, an engineer promoted the latest 1930s Lionel engines in a three-foot-high die-cut dealer counter display.

Lionel actually had its own mascot—with the symbol Lion-L as a visual pun. The lion logo first appeared in a 1913 catalog showing a young boy running his Li-

American Flyer milk glass dealer display globe: $385— Bertoia's Kuehnle Sale, 2005.

onel set on one track and the firm's latest brainchild, steel racing cars, on another track. (Racing or slot cars never really caught on with the Lionel faithful.)

Catalog centerfolds (a.k.a. gatefolds), another Lionel innovation, revealed dramatic foldouts with full-size renderings of classic Blue Comet and Brown State sets in a 1931 edition.

Over the years, Lionel commissioned America's top illustrators whose bold, stunning covers have contributed appreciably to the aesthetics as well as the collecting value of these catalogs. As Roger Carp writes in *Art of Lionel Trains: Toy Trains and American Dreams* (Kalmbach Publishing, 2003), "Analysis of the ways artists depict Lionel trains reveals much about popular values in twentieth-century America."

Vibrantly colored cardboard promotional display units for toy train dealers are highly collectable, though few survive intact. Surprisingly, at the star-studded June 2005 New England Toy Train Exchange (NETTE) auction of high-end Lionel and European train sets in Fairfield, Conn., the sale's high achiever was a five-foot store display from the early 1930s of a young lad with Santa Claus showcasing several American Flyer train sets. The festive, well-preserved display soared to a record-breaking $26,400.

Another eagerly pursued dealer display is the late-1940s "Lionel/The Giant of the Rails," an animated life-size cutout of a railroad switchman with lantern that actually swings to and fro. See also record prices set for dealer displays at Maurer's Lenhart Sale, in the Major Auction Review.

Lionel also innovated with a number of in-house publications that gave the inside scoop to its legions of customers—*Lionel* magazine in 1930, *Model Builder* in the 1940s and 1950s, and *Railroad Planning Book* in 1944. A 1950s edition of Lionel's *Toy Trains* magazine pictured sportscaster Bill Stern in a Lionel showroom layout on the cover. In 2002, *Inside Track* emerged as still another Lionel publication. All are eagerly sought by train collectors.

Late 1940s electric Lionel stand-up dealer Switchman display; lantern swings when activated.

At this point, you should hopefully be more aware of the many crosscurrents of toy train collecting opportunities that await you. It is up to you to determine what direction your collection takes, what limits you want to set, and how much fulfillment you hope to get out of it. The late Bernard Barenholtz, who introduced this writer to the hobby, once observed, "The most important reason to collect may not be intrinsic to the toys themselves, but to the wonderful people you meet all over the world, whose paths would probably never had crossed but for the sharing of this special interest." ◼

2

THE ESSENTIALS

Grading Model Trains

Whatever you collect—coins, baseball cards, mechanical banks, vintage automobiles, postage stamps, Old Masters canvases, or toy trains—the one common denominator that has a profound monetary impact on the buying, selling, and aesthetics of objects is *condition*. True value is always in the eye of the beholder, but more and more discriminating collectors place condition as their number one priority.

Whatever the venue—a garage sale, swap meet, a train emporium, a TCA convention show, or an internet or live auction, the following rigid grading standards set by TCA or other grading organizations are essential to avoid disappointment and angst; these standards bear diligent referencing in all future toy train transactions.

The mere fact that certain dealers and auction houses may use descriptions such as "pristine" and "perfect" is no assurance that you can take them at their word. Also be wary of the term "unique." Be certain that the person using it defines it as "one-of-a-kind."

- **Mint** In "as new" condition; virtually pristine or unmarred; complete and fully operable; includes original box: 10 points.
- **Like New** Between excellent and mint; may have minor paint or lithography wear; but 98 percent plus is as near as most trains get: 8 or 9 points.
- **Fine (or Excellent)** Barely perceptible scratches or nicks; no dents, rust, or fading. 90 percent intact: 6–8 points.
- **Good** Average condition with 70 percent of requisite finish: 4–6 points.
- **Poor** Less than 30 percent paint or finish; past redemption: 0–2 points.

It is recommended that any train specimen in only fair or poor condition be withdrawn from consideration, unless it is extremely rare or perhaps unique.

The hobby has another frequently used grading classification—"restored." Some examples are very clumsily done and unworthy of consideration, but there are a number of outstanding toy and train restorers in the hobby who do such a professional job that their retouching is undetectable to the naked eye. The color scheme approximates that of the original and the mechanism has been brought back to an operable stage. Knowing that vintage train sets, having been played with and given countless hours of pleasure over the years, may betray signs of wear and tear, train collectors tend to be more forgiving and condition issues bear less of a stigma than in other categories of playthings, such as mechanical banks and dolls. Of course, there will always be those purists among us who are not remotely concerned about actually playing with their trains but are, rather, obsessed with the display, giving them the white glove treatment, handling with the delicacy of a heart surgeon performing a triple bypass. As sticklers for perfection, there is the risk of missed opportunity of acquiring a truly significant, but slightly flawed specimen.

The value of a train set being intact with all parts and accessories, especially its original box or inserts, cannot be overestimated. Examples have been noted at recent train auctions where the inclusion of the box results in an added premium of at least 30 percent or higher.

The Three R's—Reproductions, Repaints, Restorations

Oh what a tangled web we weave, when first we practice to deceive.—*Sir Walter Scott*

The hobby of toy and model trains presents more of a gray area when it comes to coping with reproductions, restorations, and repaints. Railroaders tend to be more flexible and forgiving in accepting examples found in these altered states. This, of course, is a distinct departure from just about every other conceivable antique or collectible pursuit. The three R's are not only frowned upon in these other genres, but items are rigidly policed and vetted. No matter what the antique or collectible in question, unless the cosmetic touch-up or tinkering is patently obvious, its surprising how many dealers and auction houses refrain from mentioning that a flaw even exists.

Reproductions

From the very beginning, toy and scale model train makers have been notorious copycats and cloners. First of all, most classic toy trains were faithful copies of real-life trains, called prototypes. From the early 1900s, train makers such as Bing, Lionel, Ives, American Flyer, and Märklin not only produced their own trains but also supplied various parts and assemblies to one another, until the final product was so mutated that it was often anybody's guess as to who made what. Ives' 1901 O-gauge locomotive was the spitting image of Issmayer's, even down to its arched cab windows; its spoked wheels were a Märklin copy. Ives even copied Märklin's shield-shape logotype until 1905, when following Märklin's strenuous objections, they withdrew it under court order. In 1907, the short-lived American Miniature Railway Co., composed of ex-Ives employees, blatantly duplicated Ives O-gauge trains nearly to the last rivet. Between 1928 and 1930, when Lionel and American Flyer took over Ives, the line became a confusing muddle of all three makers' parts and car bodies.

Even when a train maker took precautions to patent or copyright certain innovative features such as a special coupler, truck design or power system, they were prone to be lax and let the patent expire.

Another reason reproductions pose less of a stigma is that the largest segment among toy train collectors, the modelers, are incurable tinkerers known to modify their own equipment to achieve greater authenticity and who are never satisfied until their train layouts have reached perfection.

Actually, in terms of quality, detailing, and workmanship, a number of contemporary train reproductions, both ready-mades and model kits, can hold their own, and in some cases surpass the genuine article.

The most widely copied trains are in Wide or Standard and O and S gauges. Lionel has produced its own line of repros called the Classics. Such early favorites include the No. 300 series passenger cars, the *Hiawatha* streamliner O-gauge, and the No. 384E and No. 90E steam locomotives. Other company have replicated Lionel's Blue Comet and Flying Yankee.

Current replicators include MTH Railking, Kadee, K-Line, Lifelike Products, Weaver, Williams, Spectrum, Pride Lines, Ltd., Overland, and Walthers (many of whose Web sites appear in our Manufacturers section).

Less pleased about restorations or reproductions are investment-minded or perfection-obsessed dealer/collectors who may have paid dearly for a classic original such as the Lionel 381-E, only to see its value eroded by an authentic-looking, darn good reproduction.

A case can be made for the replicators who contend that a readily affordable look-alike helps open up the hobby to those who otherwise cannot hope to compete with the deep-pocketed in vying for elusive and endangered originals.

It is only at some unspecified time in the future, when a given reproduction or altered train resurfaces to be resold, that the ethical dilemma rears its head. Entry-level collectors and even more seasoned modelers have been known to be fooled by a choice example, purported to be original, but alas, a copy.

For those who want no surprises and prefer the genuine article, there are certain guidelines to avoid being stung.

There's no substitute for knowledge and experience. Attend shows, swap meets, and exhibitions and visit any of a host of train museums, such as the TCA Museum at Strasburg, Pennsylvania.

Check and recheck catalogs and flyers; pore over the many books on the subject that illustrate and describe models in minute detail. Keep posted and watch for "repro alerts" in such publications as *Classic Toy Trains*, *Railroad Model Craftsman*, and others cited in our Train Collector Publications section.

Deal only with those in the hobby you can trust and who come recommended by fellow collectors, can provide references, and are prepared to guarantee the train's authenticity.

Should even the slightest suspicion persist, never hesitate to seek a second opinion from a trusted fellow collector or another reputable dealer.

Watch price. Any train entry that's offered at a price far below what you know to be the going rate should send up a red flag as to whether the toy is legitimate.

Never be shy about questioning the seller about his knowledge of the item, as to pedigree or track record.

Carefully examine every minute detail of the train. Are the parts indigenous to the time frame in which they were allegedly produced? Obviously a molded plastic boiler or a cowcatcher affixed to a vintage locomotive known to be of tin, brass, or cast-iron might raise a few doubts. Many of the late 1920s Dorfan locomotives that surface today, such as the No. 890 Champion Limited, have replaced body shells and trucks due to the high mortality rate of their original zinc-cast assemblies. Dorfan examples are so highly esteemed, however, that collectors are often prone to make a concession in this case. (Note: Lionel 200 and 500 series replacement trucks amply fill the bill.)

Summary

Bear in mind that the collecting of toy trains is conceived as the collecting of a factory-produced product. Your goal, therefore, is to secure and preserve specimens that are as close as possible to the condition they were in when they left the factory. This is quite a different story than finding a toy train in as close to a *simulation* of that state or condition as possible.

A moment's reappraisal will make clear the vast gap between these two concepts.

Lastly, rely on your second sense or "third eye" to determine if the train is right. This comes with time and experience in handling trains. Once you've gained more exposure and confidence, there should be no hesitation in making a buying decision.

Repaints

Repaints require more careful scrutiny than reproductions. This holds true whether the train is a new "creation" (a commemorative piece not patterned after any original from the past) or a conversion of a less scarce and desirable model or color variant to one that is feverishly pursued. There is far more cosmetic trickery afoot than meets the eye. By airbrushing, touch-up artists are known to achieve results far superior to the regular brush application.

Old or original paint has the following characteristics:

- Often shows its age by crazing (minute hairline cracks).
- Evidence exists of wear in normal wear areas; e.g., next to keywind or switch; around moving parts.

- Has a harder finish than new paint and is less likely to scratch easily.
- Appears to be a different color than new paint under black light testing; e.g., original red will appear olive green under UV light; newer red appears as bright orange.

New paint may be detected as follows:

- Often betrays its presence by odor.
- Easily scratches because of softness of finish.
- Parts of the same color match-up and will change color uniformly under black light.
- When xylene or acetone agents are applied to a tiny, less visible part, new paint quickly dissolves while old paint remains unaffected.
- Decorative detailing such as striping, lettering, and logos often appear too crisp or solid to be true.
- Older original detailing tends to appear nicked, worn, and chalky.

By closely inspecting the inside of the body shell you can usually find traces of the original colors, the result of over-spraying. This is the best indicator as to the original shell color.

Eventually, it's essential that you conduct research on various paint processes on your own. Learn the terminology of frames, over-spraying, shells, stress marks, and other nuances which provide clues as to the original vs. repaint.

Another element that has an adverse effect on a train's finish is shellacking—as it ages shellac takes on an unsightly yellow cast. The process is also irreversible.

Often in auction catalogs, dealer mail order, and eBay listings, you'll note descriptions such as "early old paint," "early restoration," or "professionally restored." What may be implied here is that the quality of the restoration is A-one and the buyer should have fewer qualms—or that the toy or model in question is the next-best compromise to the original. A general rule of thumb: A repainted or doctored specimen has 50 percent of the resale value of the all-original.

Restoration and Repair

A whole cosmos of mini-suppliers is out there offering spare wheels, trucks, frames, couplings, headlights, bells, and whistles. Walthers, the acknowledged modeler's "Bible," lists 50,000 railroad parts by more than 300 firms. For years, Approved Lionel Stations provided a service for collectors who wanted their trains repaired.

Certain repairs are not without their risks, however. Noted train consultant Ken Post, in choosing an Ives No. 1694 Passenger Set as one of his top three favorites (see chapter on Portfolio of Blue Ribbon Classics), cited a major flaw associated with that classic. Ives' output was limited to only 200 sets of tab and slot construction. Many of the Ives 1694s featured flimsy tin tabs that were inserted in slots to connect mating sections of the locomotive body. Over time, these tags were prone to snap off. As a remedy, a number of hobby shops and repair stations chose to drill holes in the shells and reattach them with screws. Ken Post estimates that 40 to 50 percent of the 1694 sets have been refitted in this way, drastically diminishing their value.

Customers seem prepared to lay out serious money for reproduction components and body shells in order to convert, revitalize, or retrofit their trains and layouts. Here again, a majority of the collectors and modelers have honorable intentions: to make the train whole again, return it to running order on the layout, or make it more presentable on the shelf or in the display case. Only a small group of devious operators undertake these alterations to pass these mutants off as unadulterated originals at inflated prices. The watchword then is to be eternally vigilant and educate yourself as to the differences between the real and the bogus. It is important to know that other safeguards do exist: The TCA requires that all repaints and repairs be duly identified on pressure-sensitive labels affixed to the item. Examples cannot be graded beyond "excellent" if the piece has been so altered. Also, any train or set that has been in rehab is subject to the rules set forth by Congress under

Public Law 93-167, the Hobby Protection Act. (This was one of the final laws enacted prior to Richard Nixon's resignation in 1974.) The act requires that any imitation of a legitimate antique or collectible be clearly marked "reproduction" in a prominent place on the object and in a nonremovable manner to prevent deception. Unfortunately, too many suspect collectors and entrepreneurs are unaware of the penalty for breaking Law 93-167, or choose to ignore it.

Custom Refinishing

There is a certain segment of the hobby who maintain that certain vintage classics of the past can be custom finished without reducing intrinsic value.

The following are a few ground rules:

- Only common trains should be customized, and true rarities should remain untouched. Relatively scarce trains in a distressed or diminished state are candidates for restoration to original colors.
- Train examples grading very good or higher should also remain unaltered.
- A custom finish should make sense aesthetically and historically.

Likely candidates include matching a caboose to a locomotive from the same set or redecorating a passenger set for a more attractive appearance than a rather drab or humdrum, flawed original.

Post Mortem

There are certain tools that a toy railroader should never be without when tracking down new acquisitions: a loupe or magnifying glass, a magnet, and a black light. A test track is also invaluable in determining if a locomotive is operable or not; many train shows, train dealers, and hobby shops routinely make them available, although it's not a convenience you're likely to find at toy auctions. Some collectors prefer to keep one step ahead and bring their own testing devices. Legendary toy and train collector Lil Gottschalk was known to carry another essential in her handbag: a bottle of smelling salts which helped pull her through many a feverish bidding duel at auction.

Creating a Complete Model Railway System

Whether you're just getting started in the hobby or are an intermediate or advanced collector, it pays to familiarize yourself with the train basics. Considering all the techno-babble dispensed by various train makers over the last hundred years, we hope that the following information will cut to the chase in helping you hook up a complete, compatible railway system. We might add that the following information is more essential to modelers—technical wizards who are known to devote years to perfecting the layout of their dreams. Most collectors and operators of toy trains tend to be less obsessed with "scale" and "gauge." They seem unfazed that liberties may have been taken to create fascinating playthings that fit on their track.

If most of this reads like Swahili, you can cheerfully ignore this chapter and put your faith in the hands of a knowledgeable, reliable fellow collector or toy train dealer, of which there are many.

Gauge and Scale

While it might appear they're one and the same (they are, in fact, often used interchangeably, in error), gauge and *scale* actually impart different meanings. All true toy railway models are miniaturized replications of real life originals known in train jargon as prototypes. As an example, an exact reduction from the original is expressed as a mathematical ratio, such as 1:87 or 1/87. This size ratio is usually expressed in fractions and is known as *scale*. The width between inner rails of track, normally predicated on the scale of the maker's line, is known as gauge. The aforementioned 1:87 scale model train is in a gauge known as HO.

Popular gauges are as follows:

- **I-gauge scale** 1¾ in. (48mm)
- **II-gauge scale** 2 in. (54mm)

- **III-gauge** 2½ in. (67mm)
- **IV-gauge** 2⅞ in. (75mm)
- **2-in. gauge** 2 in. (51mm)
- **2⅞-in. gauge** 2⅞ in. (75mm)
- **O-gauge** 1¼ in. (25mm) (A 75-foot long locomotive equates to 18½ in. in O-gauge.)
- **HO gauge** ⅝ in. (16.5 mm) (A 75-foot long locomotive is 10½ in. long in HO gauge.)
- **OO-gauge** ¾ in. (16.5mm) (European makers labeled anything smaller than O-gauge as OO.)
- **G-gauge** 1⅓ in. (48mm) (A 75 ft. loco is 40 in. long in G-gauge.)
- **N-gauge** 0.354 in. (9.0mm) (A 75 ft. long locomotive measures 5½ in. long in N-gauge.)
- **Narrow:** appeared largely in kit form; accommodates G-gauge, N-gauge, and HO-gauge model trains.
- **S-(Standard) gauge** ⅞ in. (24 mm) (A 75 ft. locomotive is 14 in. long in S-gauge.)
- **TT-gauge** 0.471 in. (11.97mm)
- **TT-gauge** 0.473 in. (12.0mm)
- **Wide gauge** ⅞ in. (24mm)
- **Z-gauge** 256 in. (6.5mm) (A 75 ft. locomotive measures 4 in. long in Z-gauge.)
- **I, II, III, IV, and OO gauge** are know to be used by European makers.
- **Standard, Wide, I, II, O, and HO gauge** have been adopted by U.S. makers over the years.

Gauges and names listed are those used by the manufacturers in their catalogs and advertisements; they are more useful for identification rather than precise measurements.

The following comparisons illustrate why gauge dimensions are for reference only, as numerous companies devised their own systems. Lionel's 2⅞ in. was compatible with European gauge 4; Carlisle & Finch's 20-in. gauges matched those of the European gauge 2. Basset-Locke and Bing's gauge 4 matched Märklin's gauge 3. Lionel's Standard gauge was theirs exclusively but equivalent to American Flyer and Ives' Wide gauge. (If this has your head spinning, join the crowd.)

Gauges shown are those used by train makers whose standards for scale were very flexible, as printed in their catalogs and advertising. There were sizeable variations in the trains running on each gauge, which can cause confusion. The above listing proves more useful for identification, as opposed to precise measurements.

Obviously, no one gauge or scale is right for everyone. It's your call as to how much space you want to devote to your trains. Do you want to run larger trains amid towering scenery? If space is at a premium, O gauge or smaller is an option. How much are your prepared to spend? The most important things is to get on track and move full speed ahead with an open mind.

Metric System
The metric system (as opposed to the English system) is used extensively, particularly among European train makers. This accounts for certain discrepancies that may be noted on the previous chart. A meter equals 39.37 inches; an inch equals 25.400 mm. To convert millimeters to inches, get out your calculator and either multiply by 0.03937 or divide by 25.4. The confusion can occur when certain train makers turn to the nearest equivalent, rounding it out in terms of an inch. Since scale is integral to gauge, we find large variations among makers as to scale as related to grade.

Whyte System
To best explain this means of deciphering a toy train wheel configuration, it is best to first define the often-misunderstood term *truck*. Keep in mind that the truck connects to a *frame* by means of a *bolster* or *support;* it includes a series of *springs* to cushion the ride and one or more *axles*. A truck, with its attached series of wheels, rotates on its axis; in later trains a combination of the truck and coupler is known as a *talgo truck*.

The *Whyte system*—a method of describing locomotive type by wheel arrangement—is employed in the U.S. and Great Britain in a numerical sequence as a standard in the hobby and applies to all types—electric and diesel, as well as steam. (As far as real-life engines are concerned, it applies only to steam-powered engines.) On the Continent, however, axles are counted instead of wheels. What we would call a 2-6-0, in Continental usage becomes a 1-3-0.

With the Whyte system, take as an example the numbers 4-6-2. The first numeral refers to number of lead wheels or pilot trucks at the front of the locomotive which smoothly guide it into a curve; in between, the second numeral refers to the power wheel truck or drivers (in this case six which propel the locomotive); the last numeral applies to the smaller trailing truck or trailers at the rear of the locomotive which guides the cab and tender in the same manner.

Railroad cars are described by the total number of wheels on a car. When a car has two trucks with four wheels to each truck, however, or six wheels in each truck, it is known as an eight-wheel car or twelve-wheel car, respectively. Actually, wheel configurations, though listed in the manufacturers' catalogs, play a lesser role in identifying a train set; more important visible clues are their *outlines,* or profiles and distinctive body shell features.

Popular Wheel Configurations

- **0-4-0** (0 pilots-4 drivers-0 trailers)
- **0-6-0** (0 pilots-6 drivers-0 trailers); e.g., the 1939 Lionel *Hudson*
- **American:** 4-4-0 (4 pilots-4 drivers-0 trailers)
- **Atlantic** 4-4-2 (4 pilots-4 drivers-2 trailers)
- **Pacific** 4-6-2 (4 pilots-6 drivers-2 trailers)
- **Planet** 2-2-2 (referring to the first British electric locomotives)
- **Outline** This term refers to the visual design characteristics of a specific toy locomotive, often distinctive to the country in which it is marketed and the type of power it uses.

Popular Outlines

American outline—typically has tall smokestack, large headlight, a bell, and no splashers or mud guards.

· **British outline** has a relatively small cab; low smokestack (funnel or chimney), a whistle, and splashers.

· **German outline** most often a large cab; occasionally has splashers.

· **Electric outline** applies to locomotives that appear to run on electricity, and were consistent with the profile or body features of true electrics of the period, but are most often clockwork-activated.

· **Steam outline** designed with large boilers, oversized stacks, assorted valves, and a steam dome; though it appears to be steam propelled, it may in fact be electric or clockwork-driven.

Wheels

In the United States, virtually all major train makers use wheels that conform to a profile called RP25. It was adopted some years ago by the National Railroad Modelers Association (N.R.M.A.). The RP25 standard not only runs well, but will also run on fine-scale track, which is more shallow than the Code 100 track standard in HO train sets.

Couplers

The device that joins each piece of rolling stock to the engine and to the other cars is called the *coupler*. Early examples were merely locking devices that held the cars together as a unit. As railroaders became more sophisticated, they pressed for ways of coupling and uncoupling automatically. Train makers came up with two types, mechanical and electric. With the mechanical, the couplers separated the cars by passing over a device in the track that physically lifted the coupler to disengage. This type proved erratic and often necessitated several passes to uncouple. Electric coupling was more selective; it required an isolated specialized segment of track, but the process could be instantly accomplished by pressing a distant controller to activate a magnetic impulse to open and disengage. The couplers could be reengaged simply by reversing the train's direction.

Special Types of Couplers

- **Automatic coupler** Based on a male–female post and slot, with each car alternating one or the other on each end for mating. Marx added this new unidirectional type coupler to its eight-wheel cars in 1938.

- **Hook coupler** First used on Ives No. 500 Series passenger cars in 1913. Ives later replaced hook couplers with automatic couplers.

- **FM-coupler** Mechanically operated knuckle coupler activated by a magnet in the disengaging section of track. Lionel, 1954–1966.

- **Link and pin** The standard coupling mechanism on American Flyer's S-gauge, with special track segment necessary for activation, beginning in the mid-1940s.

- **Eyelet system** Close-fitting system of coupling for American Flyer's Zephyr-style locomotives such as the Hiawatha.

- **T-type semi-automatic coupler** A unidirectional type located on each end of Wide-gauge American Flyer locomotives. Female section was spring-loaded scissor-type receptacle which received the male T.

- **Knuckle coupler** Method similar to the Marx one-way, or post and/or scissor automatic couplers, except that this Lionel coupler could mate in either direction without the inconvenience of having to change the direction of all the cars when going into reverse.

- **Automatic knuckle coupler** Introduced by American Flyer in 1952, although the link method continued to be the firm's most widely used coupler. Marx later came up with similar automatic coupler with a scissoring type attachment that was multidirectional.

- **Non-operating knuckle couplers** Gilbert-American Flyer first adopted this type for its cabooses in 1960 and in an economy move, outfitted it for all of its rolling stock in the years until its demise in 1967. These non-functioning couplers are for appearance only.

- **Magne-traction by Lionel and Pull-Mor by Gilbert-American Flyer** These rubber tire models were both introduced in the 1950s to increase locomotives' pulling power and traction.

Controls

Movement is what makes the world go round, or in this case, the model railway layout. The manner in which the train set and its railside equipment and buildings operate depends on the system used by the various manufacturers. Unfortunately, all the different type of locomotives and rolling stock can't be incorporated in one layout.

Most trains today are powered by electric motors and controlled through the tracks, with the current supplied to the tracks varied by the controller or transformer, a device that converts household current to safe, alternating current and low voltages. The controller regulates the speed at which the motor revolves. Gears in the motor assure you that your locomotive travels at a reasonably realistic speed.

In each instance, the current is stepped down to a safe level through the transformer. Most motors function at 12V DC, although there are exceptions.

Voltages:
United States: 110–112V AC

Great Britain: 240V AC

Germany: 220V AC

Power plants also vary, so be cautious about mixing those from various manufacturers of different countries with the original, without double-checking first with someone who knows their power sources.

Except for the pioneering days of toy trains when electric model railways ran on a three-rail track, most layouts include the two-rail, 12V DC system—the notable exception being Märklin, which runs on a 16V AC system. Two-rail direct current is by far the most common method of power supply. Most train sets come complete with at least an adequate controller unit. (Controllers can also be purchased separately.) All but the very simplest are equipped with AC/DC outputs for operating equipment.

An important caveat regarding the two-rail system: Reversing loops when a train is in a turning triangle, or return loops when a train changes direction on the same track, will not function unless special changeover or polarity-reversing switches are installed in the track circuit. Track turning on itself sets up opposite polarity, resulting in a short circuit.

Command Control

State-of-the-art computer technology, with microchips wired into the locomotive, has enabled systems to run a number of trains simultaneously without the complex wiring and sectionalizing complexity that was typical of big layouts. Scores of catalogs and flyers are available for these smart-chip locomotives, and dot-com addresses beckon to help you select your command control. One recommended source is William K. Walthers Inc.'s annual model railroad reference books, the modeler's Bible. The Milwaukee company lists over 50,000 railroad accessories made by some 300 firms.

Lionel's Trainmaster Command Control, introduced in the 1970s as a means of running up to 99 trains simultaneously, sends commands in the form of radio waves either through the outside rails or through wires. It requires routing switches and activating accessories to assume control of each unit individually. A Lionel exclusive, the Trainmaster is still being marketed, and an upgrade board is available from Train America Studios for use by postwar makers such as K-Line, MTH, Sunset, Weaver, Williams, and other three-rail firms.

Lionel's Railscope

Early in 1989, Lionel introduced a video innovation for railroaders. Railscope is a fascinating breakthrough consisting of a black and white TV camera powered by a 9V DC alkaline battery and mounted in the front end of the locomotive. This tiny camera is available for G, O, S, and HO gauges. A TV signal is transmitted via the rails back to the TV monitor to provide an engineer's view of what lies ahead on the track. For railroaders with large and complicated layouts, this allows them to safely control their trains even when they're on the other side of a mountain.

The one drawback is that it uses up more batteries than a youngster's remote control racer at Christmastime (battery life runs from 30 to 45 minutes). An enterprising modeler, with a will, finds a way. We have already heard of several different remedies, including using track power to extend battery life.

In 1999, the Grosse Pointe, Michigan, firm trading as Choochoocam marketed a monitoring device by that catchy name. The unit is a track powered three module VCR-compatible, full-color, TV-quality video camera system that can be mounted on any HO locomotive or its cars, with a transmitter and power packs (it can also be modified to fit O, G, and other gauge sets). Battery operated, it runs up to $1\frac{1}{2}$ hours without recharging. Also adding realism to the layout scene is the Choochoosound II, which transmits sound from a camera-mounted unit to a TV speaker. The device picks up the clickety-clack of track joints, crossing gate bells, whistles, and sounds of passing trains.

Digital Electronics

The German innovator Märklin has been one of the prime movers over the last decade in advancing the role of digital electronics in the hobby. By 2004, the Göppingen firm was in its third generation of digitally programmed multiple-train sets. Their current starter sets include digital decoders and controlled high-efficiency operation; they control headlights, running gear lights, smoke, and whistles, and many included a mobile hand controlled unit. For further details: www.marklin.com

Your first layout

A practical, time-proven way to get highballing down the line in model railroading is to build your first layout on a modest scale—on a 4 × 6– or 4 × 8–foot sheet of $\frac{1}{2}$-inch plywood and mount it to a simple 1 × 4–foot lumber frame. Your hobby shop or train dealer can recommend books that include track plans for small layouts. Good basic information is also found in *Beginner's Guide to N-scale Model Railroading* and

Practical Guide to HO Model Railroading, both by Kalmbach Publishing. Track is the easy part. Typically it takes six curved sections to make a half circle—usually 36 inches across in HO gauge or 19½ inches in N gauge. In HO, the straight sections are usually 9 inches long. Your dealer most likely offers additional track sections—straights, curves, and switches in various sizes—giving you the flexibility to set up your layout in just about any configuration.

There's no better way to get the feel of model railroading than by just doing it—putting your do-it-yourself skills and imagination to work. As modelers like Bruce Zaccagnino and Bruce Chubb can confirm, great layouts are built one step at a time.

Housing and Showcasing Your Trains
Take your pleasure seriously—*Charles Eames*

One of the joys of collecting toy trains is the many options for storing, displaying, and running your treasures. There are those who literally "live" their hobby, turning their quarters into one giant layout with mazes of track leading from room to room. More than one modeler has purchased a particular home because it featured a commodious attic, game room or basement with wide open spaces for benchwork, layouts, and consists. These people tend to be techies, fixated on the tiniest detail, and many are highly artistic as well. They install state-of-the-art sound systems and incorporate computerized commands into their computer or electronic systems, and have the satisfaction of being in control of an entire system of railroads. Although all manner of train kits, power packs, and thousands of parts are available, many layouts are scratch-built. Modelers become so consumed, it matters little that their layouts are forever "works in progress," and represent commitment to spend ten to twenty years perfecting their layouts.

A entirely different breed, known as '"live steamers," build oversized steam locomotives they can ride outdoors (known as garden trains) and are dismissed by scale modelers as "those darn machinists."

On the opposite pole, there are some people who seem perfectly content to follow a time-honored family ritual of running the set under the Christmas tree once a year.

With the current mania for Lilliputian scale trains such as O, HO, Z, and N gauges, die-hard miniaturists can eschew the luxury of a lot of space; they divert their efforts toward acquiring more track and scaled-down scenery, and transcend mechanical concerns with their appreciation of the milieu in which railroads operated. Jim Doherty, in an article in *Smithsonian Magazine* in December 1988, tells about an O-scaler who grumped that one could build a Z-scale railroad on the brim of a straw hat, "but the darn thing is so small that when you want to get a closer look, your nose knocks it off the track."

Then, of course, there's the "closet collector"—the accumulator who is content to keep his treasures under wraps, stashed away in crates and boxes and available for inspection when and if the inclination arises.

With feet firmly planted in the middle of all this melange, the pure toy train fancier is the type you're most likely to spot at a toy show or auction. He is a fountain of knowledge and can recite the complexities of engine numbers, gauges, wheel configurations, outlines, and color variants as if it were a second language. Track is a secondary concern to these collectors, most of whom are content to show off their prizes on open shelves or in gleaming display cases, preferably accompanied by their original boxes. How a train collection should be displayed is strictly a matter of individual taste, personality, imagination, and creative flair, but most collectors strive to convey a feeling of nostalgia for a certain time and place. A number of prominent vintage toy and train collectors over the years—Bernard Barenholtz, Bill Holland, Ward Kimball, Rich and Lil Gottschalk, and Dave Peters Sr., to name a few—were known for creating evocative settings in their homes that seamlessly intermingled toy trains with folk art, paintings, and railroadiana.

Exhibiting trains in open display areas can be a great pleasure, but it does have some drawbacks—dust, humidity, and direct sunlight—all of which take their toll on the trains.

Showing off trains in the best light

To avoid overexposure to these harmful side effects, many collectors wisely rotate their train displays, keeping those not on view well protected in boxes and bags or in special climate-controlled, Plexiglas drawers and cases. To avoid the harmful rays of ultraviolet light, low-wattage mini-shelf lights, available in hobby shops or on eBay, are recommended. They show off trains to their best advantage without distorting colors and tones, or making it difficult to distinguish color variants. Fluorescent lighting, another option, tends to give a different cast to an object. Treated Plexiglas is another way to block off UV rays, which can lead to fading or foxing. It is also advisable to set up your train displays in a portion of the room where daily exposure to sunlight is minimal.

Other precautions

Make a periodic cleaning schedule for your trains and stick to it. Cast-iron and other cast-metal engines and cars should not be cleaned with soap, detergent solutions, or water, even on paint that has been permanently bonded. Instead, apply a cloth dipped in a few drops of light machine oil and exert very little pressure when cleaning. Plastic cars and parts are sometimes adversely affected by certain machine oils so always check first with your local dealer or hobby shop owner as to a proper lubricant. Lithographed tin trains can normally be cleaned safely with water and a mild detergent such as Murphy's Oil Soap. If any doubt arises about the material being cleaned, dip a cotton swab in a cleaning mixture and test a small, less noticeable area of the train first before cleaning the more visible parts. Light machine oil should also be applied periodically to any moving parts to keep your cars running smoothly and quietly.

Above all, know what you don't know and never hesitate to seek outside guidance. The pros at train shows, museums, and conservation centers are there to give you the benefit of their experience.

Dismantle or "field strip" and inspect engines, cars, and accessories at least once a year to determine if there are any signs of rust, pitting, or other problems, then take immediate remedial steps. Avoid handling your trains as much as possible. A single fingerprint has been known to etch metal, and oil from the skin can smudge vintage finishes.

When packing trains

One of the preferred methods of storing lighter-weight rolling stock is to fold each unit in a slightly larger cloth bag, allowing enough of the bag to overlap and protect each car fore and aft as well. Heavier locomotives, or those with fragile extensions such as pantographs, ladders, and headlights can be wrapped in bubble wrap or packing foam. (P.G.A. golfer Ed Dougherty, in a *Classic Toy Trains* article, admitted to swathing some of his favorite F3 silver cars in silk sheets for protection, something he didn't even have on his own bed.)

Stack bagged cars in sturdy cardboard or wooden boxes (the type now readily available for Christmas tree ornaments really do the trick.) Pack items three layers deep, with the heavier locos and cars on the bottom, of course. Second- and third-tiered cars are best turned on their sides to prevent flanged wheels or other projections from poking into the cars beneath. Refrain from packaging your trains in newsprint or other makeshift wrapping materials. Inks and acids contained in newsprint and plastics can prove harmful.

We recommend a dehumidifier if the storage area is subject to temperature changes or is occasionally damp. In small enclosures, collectors and dealers frequently rely on crystal desiccants used by jewelers and tobacconists to reduce moisture. At the very least, use a relative humidity indicator in the area to monitor changes. Adequate ventilation is also critical.

On concrete floors, which tend to retain moisture, boxes should rest on wooden frames or casters. Ideally, artifacts are best stored in darkness, so each box or container should be covered. This is essential for such ephemera as train catalogs, timetables, and any accessories made of paper or cardboard.

Inventorying and Insuring Your Collection

Another concern is how to safeguard your investment from natural disasters, as well as fires or burglary. Few dealers and collectors have the resources to evacuate their inventory in the time of crisis; they are, understandably, more concerned with evacuating their families in the face of high winds, floods, or wildfires. But proper insurance coverage can guarantee that even if your trains are lost, your investment is not.

The first step is to consider the kinds of insurance coverage you should have in the event of a disaster. Check to see that your policy covers the types of natural disasters to which your region falls victim, from flooding to mudslides. Can your collection be covered by a standard homeowner's policy, or do you need an additional personal collection policy? Your insurance agent will be able to help you with these questions.

The most important thing is to secure thorough computerized documentation of each and every item in your possession. In the event of a loss, you can at least file a claim, but adjusting it would be quite a problem if you lack proof of what was in your gallery, in storage, or in your personal collection. Protect your records: Keep a back-up disk at a separate location, or take disks of your files with you.

Insurance companies love receipts of what you've paid for an item, backed up by a photographic record. We know of any number of collectors who have purchased video cameras and methodically documented each article for posterity.

It is also advisable that you completely evaluate your insurance protection as it relates to the area where you live. Arrange a meeting with your insurance agent so that every aspect of your policy is clear in your mind. In recent years, homeowner's and also renter's policies have become more comprehensive in coverage.

Ray Haradin, a noted militaria and mechanical bank dealer/collector, writes in *Old Toy Soldier*: "The dichotomy of insurance is, if you fully insure your collection, the high premiums you pay generally offset the appreciation value of your collection." Haradin still recommends insurance, and in many instances your collection can be covered under the contents portion of your homeowner's policy.

Although the rates vary, the industry generally assumes that antiques and collectibles appreciate at five percent each year. They will compare this value, based on your receipts, with the appraised value. Should a large discrepancy exist between adjusted purchase price and appraisal value, a professional appraiser should be called in.

Another option is to purchase a fine arts rider (also called a floater or endorsement) to a standard homeowner's policy. This rider can insure selected artifacts at predetermined values. It's well worth the added outlay because your treasures can be insured at true value—which can be increased to adjust to the prevailing market. Further, the rider is not subject to deductible or depreciation allowances, as often occurs with homeowner's policies. Fine arts riders can usually be negotiated; provisions are less restricted than with regular policies.

In recent years, a number of collecting organizations have banded together with the Association of Collecting Clubs to sponsor insurance programs that offer distinct advantages and savings. Coverage is administered by the AIA, the Association Insurance Administrators, a Best's-rated, A+ insurance company, one of the world's largest. No appraisals are required. Only single items over $2,500 need be listed on the application. Rates are very affordable and the replacement cost coverage will be paid at the current market retail value at time of loss. It is truly "all risk" insurance, covering fire, lightning, windstorm, vandalism, theft, vehicle overturn, accidental breakage, flood, earthquake, and shipping coverage. It carries a $250 deductible (5 percent wind deductible in Florida). This policy does not cover dealer inventory, but dealer insurance programs are available through the A.I.A. Web site: AntiqueAndCollectible.com

Buying and Selling Trains at Auctions and eBay

Buying at Auction

Whether you're in the gallery or on real time (bidding live) on the phone or eBay, auctions seem to serve as an ideal venue for adding new prizes to your collection. By the same token, most consignors swear that going the auction route is the most painless way to get a maximum return on your toy train investment. But buying and selling trains at auction can be a bit more complicated than toy, doll, or bank auctions. The procedure is often quite similar to auctions of antiquarian books; multiples of a specific maker or category may be sold as a "lot," or "lotted," and the value, desirability, and condition of each item included in that lot may vary drastically. Train auctioneers also tend to move along at a much faster pace. When trains come up, on occasion, in the context of a general auction, estimates tend to be unrealistic and condition discrepancies overlooked. On the other hand, if the item proves to be a rare find, your chances of winning it are enhanced if your railway rivals are not in on the action.

When Attending the Auction

It behooves you, as a potential bidder, to visit the auction preview and allow yourself ample time to examine each lot carefully. Arriving early allows time for a thorough, unhurried inspection, before the crowd converges, and enables you, should the need arise, to confirm the vintage of the train or arrange with the auction manager to have an item put up at a certain time (providing it's not a cataloged sale).

Auction Terminology

Although many auction terms are self-explanatory, it's still important to be aware of the various intricacies or legalese a sale entails.

- **Absolute sale** Any auction is which every item in the sale will be sold without a reserve.

- **Bidding pool** Group of dealers or collectors who pre-determine that one member will bid for the group. To keep the hammer price low, they won't compete against one another. They later convene (usually outside the gallery) and conduct their own private silent auction. The winner then compensates his fellow conspirators, based on their respective underbids. Needless to say, auctioneers and consignors alike are not happy about the lot selling at a deflated value. The practice is now illegal in many states.

- **Bid increments** May vary by auction house, but they are pre-set and listed in the catalog or shown on-line in an auction's overview page and reiterated by the auctioneer at the sale's onset. If, for instance, the bid increment is 10 percent and the current bid on a lot is $900, the next bid would be $990, a jump of $90. As you go up in the five figures bracket, say $10,000, the next bid would be $11,000—a more substantial raise of $1,000.

- **Catalog sale** Most major auction houses issue elaborate, fully illustrated catalogs or at least a printed listing that carefully describe each lot in the sale, with estimates and the order in which each item will be sold.

- **Ceiling bid** The best way for absentee bidders to win a desired lot is to submit a ceiling bid that is clearly on the high side and the maximum amount they're prepared to pay. This by no means implies that you'll ultimately pay that amount. It only enhances your chances of winning your prize train model. Most house rules dictate that should you wind up with the top bid, it will not exceed that of the next highest bidder by 10 percent or at most, 20 percent. Morphy Auctions co-founder Dan Morphy reported that in his September, 2005 Auction, there was an instance where one bid was left for a maximum of $25,000, but the fortunate bidder eventually won the item for $2,200. Even so, prepare yourself for the contingency that someone out there may be more fixated on owning the item than you are.

- **Estimate** Ideally, it's usually listed as a low and high estimate of the expected price each lot will bring, determined by the auction house and hopefully based on previous sales or track record of similar items.

- **Fair warning** Your signal from the auctioneer that the bidding is about to close, and if still interested in the item, act now or it's going, going, gone.

- **Lot** Consists of one item or a group of items that are sold together.

- **One times money** Also known as one times bid, applies when individual lots are placed in a group, requiring a bid for the entire group. The winning bid also claims all items from said group, and by its very nature, no absentee bids can be entertained, even if the absentee bid has been placed on any lot in that group. Depending on the arrangement with consignor, the auctioner then has the option to sell each item separately. Fortunately this crops up only occasionally.

- **Preemptive bid** A legitimate tactic that jump-starts the action with a large bid; it's an attempt to intimidate competitive buyers that seldom scares off the competition.

- **Reserve price** The lowest price at which the consignor is willing to sell a lot. This price is generally higher than the minimum opening bid.

- **To the order** Term an auctioneer announces to indicate that he's executing a written bid on behalf of an absent bidder. Auction houses cannot execute "buy" bids (those that assert the bidder is prepared to top all buyers).

Sam Pennington in a recent *Maine Antique Digest* editorial writes, "Everyone knows that there are at least three different kinds of appraisals—low for real estate tax purposes, high for insurance replacement value, and in the middle for willing buyer/willing seller." The late auctioneer Robert Skinner once explained that, in his view, estimates reflected the expectation of the consignor. He said he felt comfortable with low estimates and thought they created excitement among bidders. Pennington poses the question, "When an auctioneer boasts that many of his lots sold for ten times their estimates, do we entrust our property to him because he's such a good auctioneer, or do we steer clear because he obviously does not know his values?"

If you read between the lines, estimates can sometimes reveal a lot. In New York City, for instance, the law states that reserves can be no higher than the low estimate. The theory is that if the reserve price was higher than the low estimate, then the auctioneer was not being truthful about your shot at buying the item at the low estimate. No other venue has adopted this law, although many auctioneers do it as a matter of policy.

When a major auction house holds a marquee train auction, as evidenced by such epic events as the recent Ward Kimball, Richard Kughn, and Gerald Poch auctions, avail yourself in advance of the elaborate, lavishly illustrated catalogs (some—e.g, the Kimball Sale—even include CDs). Catalogs are usually priced at $30 to $35 and prove to be well worth the investment, as they (a) help determine if it's worth your time and energy to attend; (b) provide presale estimates as a guideline; and (c) serve, along with postsale prices realized, as a handy reference for buying and selling at future auctions and shows. Most houses also post digital images of top entries on their Web site previews which can be downloaded. Also, don't be hesitant about calling, faxing, or e-mailing the auction house contact for any clarification or doubts you might have as to provenance and condition. It could save major headaches later.

Be certain to find a seat or place to stand in the gallery with an unobstructed view of the podium so you can be readily spotted by the auctioneer. Make positive bidding motions. Some bidders are known to drive auctioneers to distraction by going though all manner of method-acting machinations such as winking, shoulder tics, barely perceptible nods, and paddle signals to indicate a bid (as if to hide their intentions from competitive bidders). The danger is, they may well fake out the auctioneer in picking up one's bid.

Contain your excitement and keep your cool by taking a few deep breaths between bids. Try not to raise your own bid; most auctioneers are usually charitable about this, but we know of others who'll leave you up there, well beyond what you should be paying. If you're uncertain as to who has the high bid, be assertive and ask the auctioneer. One piece of advice that's easier said than done: Decide in advance the absolute maximum you're prepared to pay, and stick to your guns.

Don't be intimidated by a so-called bidding pool, mentioned earlier. Remember that those participating in the pool need some slack to resell the item for a profit. As auctioneers are quick to point out, as long as the pool is still bidding against you, in all probability, the price of the lot remains in the realm of reason.

Bidding Absentee
There may be occasions when you simply can't personally attend the auction. Most auction houses provide the option of participating as a phone bidder, entering a left bid as an absentee bidder by mail or fax, or being part of the live bidding action on eBay.

When submitting your mail bid, some auction houses require a deposit (usually 20 percent.) Another alternative is to appoint a proxy, preferably someone you know to be ethical and assertive who knows his trains, who would be willing (usually for a fee) to bid on your behalf. (We've seen certain proxies at auction entertain bids for any number of clients, juggling a handful of paddles like semaphores.)

Selling at Auction
The consignor or seller's role at auction is so often cloaked in technical jargon and fine print that most dealers and collectors are more comfortable buying than selling at auctions. This unease is due to the seller being relegated to a silent partner in the auction process. Once the seller has consigned his property to the auction house, his participation usually

ceases. Before you sign a contract, make certain that the auction house describes each lot accurately, with any flaw or missing part clearly noted.

Make certain you have a thorough comprehension of the commission arrangement and any hidden extras are spelled out to your satisfaction. Auction houses are known to charge varying commission rates to consignors and some assess extra fees for services and expenses incurred, such as transportation, insurance, photography, cataloging, advertising, and repairs. Seller's commissions will vary from house to house, depending on how the contract is negotiated. Normally the rate is 10 to 25 percent, depending on whether there is a buyer's premium. Buyer's premiums or add-ons are the amount paid out by the buyer for his purchase, a percentage of the final price. For example, if a bidder wins a lot at $2,000, he owes an additional $200 to the house (10 percent of the winning bid). A recent auction trend applies to high-end lots that may exceed $100,000; the house factors in the premium in descending scale as the item escalates. (An example: A buyer add-on is 15 percent up to and including $100,000, and drops to 10 percent of the balance owed beyond that amount.) Certain major auction houses, most notably in the fine arts genre, have been known to waive a seller's fee entirely for the prestige and publicity of handling a world-class collection.

To protect your investment, you might wish to discuss selling your consignment subject to reserve. In order to win the item, a bidder must meet or exceed the reserve price and entertain the highest bid. If no bidders meet that reserve, neither the seller nor the high bidder are under further obligation to complete the transaction. As seller, however, you may still be out of pocket if your contract with the auction house stipulates that you've authorized the house to act as exclusive agent for 60 days following the auction to sell the property for the previously agreed reserve price.

A growing trend among certain major auction houses is to hold so-called absolute auctions in which there are no reserves. Some detractors feel this is akin to working without a safety net, but actual auction results bear out that entries of proven pedigree and ultimate rarity tend to seek their own level. Ron Bourgeault of Northeast Auctions even forgoes estimates, except on reserved lots. This leads to spirited competition as bidders know the goods are there to be sold.

Compensation

Consignors can expect to be paid, minus seller's commission and set fees, as soon as buyers have paid your auction house. Normally this is 35 days after the gavel falls.

Buying and Selling on eBay

"Going, going, gone, sold to cyberspace." It's hard to believe that six years have passed since auctioneer Tim Luke spoke that immortal refrain at the Bertoia's Poch Sale Part II in Philadelphia, in October 1999, their first venture into eBay. Today, at most major auction houses, eBay plays a pivotal role in stimulating the bidding process. Those actually attending a live event are known to grouse about cyberspace slowing down the bidding action. Auction houses, however, love the added competition for their wares, and many attest that eBay brings a new breed of more youthful collectors into the mix.

The gathering horde of those who buy and sell on eBay is more than 60 million users at last count. The step-by-step procedures in bidding on eBay live are clearly spelled out the second you log in. More and more dealers and collectors are choosing cyberspace for the convenience of not having to leave your house. Only registered eBay users who have signed up for the auction can bid live. It's easy to become a registered user by placing a credit card on file or by presenting an alternative ID via Equifax. Your credit card will not be charged; it's on file for identification only. Registering is not necessary if you wish to browse and follow a sale's progress.

Feedback Forum is a vital eBay convenience that enables users to instantly verify the track record or business practices of anyone at eBay. The forum is a place where users leave comments about each other's reputation in the buying and selling experience.

For a definitive resource for first-time users and on-line pros, *The Official eBay Bible* (Gotham Books, NYC) is highly recommended. ◨

3

TOY AND MODEL TRAIN HISTORY

Milestones in Toy Train Evolution

The evolution of the toy train from the 1840s to the present day is, for many train manufacturers, a fascinating roller-coaster ride taken by a relatively obscure, family-owned company to find their niche in European, American, and later, worldwide markets. The era of the toy train extends to nearly a century-and-a-half—and counting. During that span, the concept of the toy train has gone through many phases, some more fascinating than others, with a continuing quest for realism as the common thread.

The Leipzig Toy Fair—1891

Gebrüder Märklin sparked a new concept in toy trains in 1891, when the Göppingen firm introduced a exhibit at the Leipzig Toy Fair. Prior to this time (as mentioned in an earlier chapter, What to Collect), most manufacturers in America as well as Europe tended to issue only locomotives and tenders rather than complete train sets; most were trackless and without railside accessories such as train stations, bridges, and tunnels. The stunning diorama, in complete scale, featured entire train sets running on a figure-eight track layout and encompassed Lilliputian passengers, terminals, trestles, bridges, signals, casinos, kiosks, and even comfort stations. The exhibit proved an unqualified success and thus was born an enlightened concept—that a toy train was not a separate entity, but an integral part of a total rail system or layout. Now train enthusiasts could continually add matching rolling stock, ready-to-install tracks, and realistic miniature buildings and railside accessories to their layouts and broaden their domain.

Concurrently, Märklin shrewdly launched a series of clockwork standard gauge models, numbered 1, 2, and 3, and after a few years, Small gauge. This way, Märklin could challenge Issmayer and other German makers who had already established a significant foothold in smaller gauge trains.

World War I—German Dominance Ends

By 1902, German firms were major importers of toy trains to the American, French, and English markets. On these shores, firms such as Bing tended to copy the outlines in I and O gauge, but with better proportions and more intricate castings. In 1905, Carette introduced steam and clockwork versions of the Baldwin *Vauclain Compound* 4-4-0, acclaimed by many experts as the handsomest American outline locomotive ever made.

Bing stuck to its gauge II and IV trains during the early 1900s and improved their quality to challenge mighty Märklin, but Bing still could not compete with them in terms of variety and range of accessories.

The two German giants still considered Ives as their only true competition on the U.S. scene, failing to note an ominous cloud on the horizon—the upstart Lionel. Great strides had been made by maverick Joshua Lionel Cowen, who ignored the traditional gauge II and christened his 2½-inch nonstandard orphan, Standard gauge. Strictly electric, Lionel sets were massive, heavy, and simply constructed. Most important, the sets were offered at the lowest price available.

World War I signaled the death knell for major German makers, as most if not all production was diverted to munitions. An early casualty, Georges Carette, a French emigre, was deported from Germany in 1917 and his factory confiscated. Other German makers, dazed and confused after the war, suffered from inflated labor and shipping costs and protectionist tariffs.

In 1920 Bing's new I-gauge, cast-iron, eight-wheel electrics proved too little too late as they couldn't match up with Lionel's Standard gauge and gradually faded from the American scene.

Plans for Märklin's top-shelf gauge II had to be abandoned for the war effort, a major loss to future collectors, judging from a tempting preview of specimens illustrated in their 1919 catalog. Heavy competition from Great Britain's Whitanco, Brimtoy, Chad Valley, and especially Hornby, along with giant strides made stateside by Lionel, Ives, American Flyer, and Dorfan, precipitated the end of the German monopoly.

The American Toy Boom and Bust— 1920–1930

In the 1920s, Joshua Cowens' greatest coup, Standard gauge, emerged as the yardstick against which, all other gauges were measured. Since Lionel owned the copyright on the designation "Standard," Ives adopted Wide gauge. Lionel reached its zenith in toy train production with the massive Blue Comet and State sets plus its most imposing steam locomotive, the Standard gauge #400E. By 1925, Lionel's coaches were offered in a wide assortment of colors and embellished with brass trim, ran on 2¼-inch track, which allowed for taller, wider and "heftier" appearance than any of their gauge-I competitors—Bing, Märklin, and Ives.

Ives, in a survival mode by the mid-1920s, initiated an ambitious, well-conceived program using 4-4-2 bipolar-type electric locomotives. They used die-castings and an advanced ball-bearing motor, with new 21-inch passenger coaches. Ives, however, was undercapitalized, and the set never really got off the drawing board. Ives declared bankruptcy in 1928. They went on to enjoy a two-year reprieve under the flagship name, while in receivership by American Flyer and Lionel. The line soon morphed into a hodgepodge of Ives, AF, and Lionel parts and equipment. With AF and Lionel beset by troubles of their own, they withdrew their support, sending Ives to raildom's Valhalla in 1932.

AF, which had dabbled earlier in the low-end market with Ives- and Bing-style windups, made an ill-advised plunge in 1925 to market cast-iron engines with lithographed coaches in Britain under the name British Flyer. The line bombed. That same year, AF went to Wide gauge and added Lionel-style coaches dressed in their own livery AF's Wide-gauge entries, larger and lower priced, proved worthy competitors to Lionel.

In 1926, Dorfan, an enterprising Newark, N.J., maker, introduced a die-cast line powered by tall, art-deco-styled locomotives. Dorfan quickly proved that in terms of sheer power, their locomotives could outperform the field. Dorfan's fatal flaw—its zinc cast engine shell—soon betrayed signs of metal fatigue and many had to be scrapped.

Just after the big stock market crash in 1929, the NYC toy maker Boucher, saddled with outmoded designs (with the exception of a Blue Comet), wisely opted out of toy trains and returned to its original ship modeling pursuits.

1930 Doldrums to World War II Recovery
Dorfan offered a small selection of appealing O-gauge trains in the late 1920s. Strapped for funds, they were compelled to produce lower quality trains during the Depression and were in a survival mode until their ultimate demise in the mid-1930s.

Louis Marx & Co. embarked on its toy train venture in 1927 with the popular Joy Line, produced under a license agreement with Girard Model Works of Albion,

Pa. After acquiring Girard in the mid-1930s, Marx produced its most exemplary set, the *Commodore Vanderbilt* locomotive with six-inch cars in various colors. The *Vanderbilt* enjoyed a long run, from 1935 into the 1970s. Marx's most coveted set among collectors, the Army Supply train in olive livery, made its debut in 1939.

In 1922, Lionel had opened a design and tooling firm in Naples, Italy, the Società Meccanica La Precisa. In keeping with their flamboyant Italian styling, Lionel in 1928 produced a popular new modified version of the Hellgate Bridge accessory. In 1932 they added more Standard-gauge coaches to the Steven Girard deluxe set.

It was "a case of too many standard gauges chasing too few dollars," according to Pierce Carlson in his definitive book *Toy Trains* (see Bibliography). After four years of bleeding "red ink," Lionel went into receivership in 1935. A Mickey Mouse clockwork handcar, introduced in 1934, had temporarily bailed them out, but despite a brief reprise, Lionel soon abandoned the cheaper, lower-profit handcar novelties. Later that year, Lionel astutely capitalized on the popularity of the real-life streamliners with three sizes of O-gauge models of the Union Pacific's *City of Portland*, which became the toast of the hobby. The "torpedos," as they were called, literally propelled Lionel out of receivership.

In 1936, American Flyer rushed in with streamliners of their own, epitomized by the Milwaukee Road's *Hiawatha*. Although AF entries were quite handsome, they took a back seat to Lionel as far as quality for the money. In 1938, under the reign of A.C. Gilbert, the inventor of the widely popular Erector Set, the old Wide gauge line was scuttled. An HO entry appeared in Gilbert's 1939 catalog and 3:16 scale took over. AF's intricately detailed die-castings and superb proportion proved a cut above Lionel's O-27's, and the Chicago firm, newly relocated to New Haven, Connecticut, was truly reborn.

Fittingly, the end of the era coincided with Lionel's 1939 introduction of a highly detailed die-cast series to appeal the fast growing number of scale model enthusiasts. The scale model series included an O-gauge switcher teamed with a New York Central 4-6-4 *Hudson* with matching freight cars. Testing the waters with O gauge proved auspicious for Lionel, as they recouped their tooling costs in less than a year. The *Hudson* achieved an unparalleled standard of realism. Unfortunately, World War II interrupted the promising development of super-scale trains.

Märklin, after a prolonged recovery period following World War I, made rapid strides in the 1930s. Adding to their heralded Reichsbahn steam outline series, Märklin increased production of superb electrics, highlighted in 1933 with the Swiss Crocodile colossus in gauge I and gauge O. Märklin, the last holdout in I gauge, at long last dropped it for gauge O in 1938. Märklin's dynamic series of international glamour locomotives in 1936 may well be the costliest, most challenging series for collectors to complete. The magnificent seven includes a (U.S.) streamlined 4-6-4 *Hudson*, a *Commodore Vanderbilt*, a non-streamline 4-6-4 *Hudson*, the French Etat Mountain 4-8-2 British L.N.E.R. *Cock o' the North*, the German *Borsig* 4-6-2, and the Swiss *Crocodile*.

In 1935, Märklin unveiled a OO-gauge *Tischbahn*, or table railroad, just in time for the Christmas season. The first foray into OO-gauge had come from Trix in 1933, just six months prior to Karl Bub buying them out, after the line failed to revitalize lagging sales. Train sets bearing Bing and Bub trademarks were offered in the low-end Nuremberg Style with indifferent results.

World War II Hiatus and Postwar Recovery

World War II disrupted the hopes and plans of countless European makers. Märklin's assets were confiscated by Germany and its factory retooled to produce munitions. Karl Bub's factory in Nuremberg was bombed on several occasions. The facilities of Trix and Gunthermann were decimated in bombing raids. In 1939, the French maker Jouets en Paris (J.E.P.) was busily tooling-up for their own HO system, but the war intervened and J.E.P. shelved their

HO's until the late 1940s. Lionel, under government contract from 1942 to 1946, switched from toy train production to Navy navigational devices for the duration.

In Europe, Märklin, at the end of the war, had a 65-year investment in OO/HO gauge, and they returned to it as soon as they could. In 1947, Märklin faithful received a long overdue treat. They resurrected the 1933 Swiss Ce6/8 *Crocodile*, this time, in OO. The miniature version joined Märklin's large gauge predecessors as a true classic. The Model V-200, their first diesel locomotive, made its debut in 1957. By the mid-1950s, Märklin was the sole survivor of the early German toy train makers. Now a giant among scores of smaller low-profile makers, Märklin has adopted the "less is more" dictum and added the widely acclaimed MAXI/I gauge and Z gauge. Today, it can well justify its claim as "world leader in model railroading."

By the early 1950s, collectors in the U.S. were laying out serious money to the tune of a million train sets a year. The standing joke was that while most purchases were presumably for young lads, it was the father who soon took over as chief dispatcher, conductor, and engineer.

Among U.S. manufacturers, Marx made a postwar resurgence in 1949. To match its carry-over inventory of the popular ³⁄₁₆-inch rolling stock, they introduced an electric of the same scale, #33, 4-6-2, one of the classiest die-cast locomotives in Marx's repertoire. A year later, they made further inroads with a Santa Fe Diesel in ¼ scale, with two back-to-back diesel engines. Though a clockwork set, Marx's *Mickey Mouse Meteor* set, 1950–1951, with colorful images of Disney denizens, became one of the hottest postwar sellers. After a less than successful venture into HO gauge, their fortunes flagged and the firm was bought out by Quaker Oats in 1972 and renamed Marx Toys. Indifferent management spelled further disaster, and Marx ended its 60-year run in 1976.

Lionel's postwar years have been hailed by most authorities as their golden era. By 1952, Lionel had single-handedly eclipsed the entire production of the nation's real-life railroads. The company produced 622,209 engines and 2,460,764 freight and passenger sets with freight outselling passenger sets by 20 to 1. Lionel nimbly managed to stay one step ahead of AF by finding new cost-cutting innovations. To the dismay of many purists, Lionel went to cheaper materials, including Bakelite and other plastics. The 1950s witnessed a series of ingenious Lionel peripherals including knuckle couplers, realistic smoke units, a battery-powered diesel horn, and magnetized wheels and axles.

In the postwar period, A.C. Gilbert–owned AF switched from HO and 3:16 scale, to miniature precisely scaled S-gauge trains that operated on a two-rail system. From 1946 to 1956, AF soared with record sales. Then came a glut on the market of lower-priced HO gauge and the entire industry felt the pinch.

When A.C. Gilbert died in 1961, Jack Wrather, owner of the *Lone Ranger* TV series, bought out AF. Wrather lacked a magic silver bullet; he drastically curtailed inventory and production. Though sales increased 30 percent in 1965, profits were offset by borrowed capital and overhead costs. A year later, Lionel, its worthy competitor for over 60 years, bailed out American Flyer.

Great Finds and Collections

The correct question on the quiz show *Jeopardy* under the category "magnificent obsessions"—a common bond among kings and maharajahs, clergymen, professors, scientists, statesmen, schoolboys, titans of business and industry, and people from all walks of life—is: Who collects toy and model trains?

Celebrity collectors past and present include: ex-Harvard president James Conant; stripper Gypsy Rose Lee; comedians Garry Moore, Jack Benny and Rochester, Arthur Godfrey, Gary Coleman, Paul Winchell and Jerry Mahoney; musicians Bing Crosby, Frank Sinatra, Mel Torme, Paul Whiteman, and Tommy Dorsey; actors Robert Montgomery and Yul Brynner; cowboys Gene Autry and Roy Rogers; boxer Gene Tunney; swimmer Johnny Weissmuller; baseball greats Joe DiMaggio, Roy Campanella, and Gil McDougald; P.G.A. golfer Ed Dougherty; former Secretaries of State John Foster Dulles and George Marshall; King Ananda of Siam; Britain's kings George VI, Edward II, and Edward VIII; and several members of the current British royal family.

Talk show hostess Opah Winfrey was a significant Internet buyer of trains at Bertoia's Poch Sale in 1999, and the auction action aired on her program some months later.

While in the White House, President Dwight Eisenhower and his wife Mamie set up Lionel sets under the Christmas tree for grandson David. Later, Lionel officials visited Eisenhower in the oval office and awarded him a special presentation model of their famous *General* locomotive and tender.

Playwright Ben Hecht delighted in staging train wrecks on his layout, and then untangled them with his Lionel crane car.

Frank Sinatra was never too far from his Hoboken, New Jersey, roots, even though residing a continent away. The singer commissioned a local hobby shop owner to recreate a large elaborate train layout of his native Hoboken in his California home that brought back fond memories of his youth.

Charles and Ray Eames, probably the most renowned design partnership of the twentieth century, were avid collectors of toy trains, boats, marionettes, and all the paraphernalia that went with them. Their collecting passion inspired them to produced a number of short films: *Traveling Boy*, with a background of Saul Steinberg drawings in 1955; *Parade* and *Toccata For Trains*, both in 1957; and *Tops* (spinning tops) in 1969. *Parade* and *Toccata*, with score by Elmer Bernstein, won a number of international awards. These films, fortunately, are still available today and are highly recommended. E-mail: gallery@eamesoffice.com.

Robert P. Monaghan, author of *Greenberg's Guide to Märklin OO/HO,* is also creator of the Märklin Museum of Philadelphia. Monaghan has spent a lifetime playing with and researching trains, and his boyhood trains were Märklin clockwork models. As an adult, he built a huge layout and over the years has opened his display to area children each Christmas, with some 3,000 attending the event.

Vincent Astor, one of many affluent collectors in the past, once had an outdoor train layout on his front lawn in Rhinebeck, New York, and another miniature track at his Bermuda estate. One of the posh American model-train fancier clubs in NYC before the financial crash of 1929 boasted seven multimillionaires among its members. After the crash, one did himself in, but the other six members, who had lost their millionaire status, still remained loyal railroaders.

High-Tech Railroaders

If you're really into the intricacies of spectacular layouts, the closest approximation of real railroading there is, here are a few role models: We first wrote about Bruce Chubb, a Grand Rapids, Michigan, electrical engineer and modeler extraordinaire, fifteen years ago. At that time, his highly sophisticated Sunset Valley Railroad computer-operated layout was capable of operating 16 trains simultaneously. Chubb meticulously printed out car-switching lists and monitored movements of individual trains and cars. When catching up with Chubb in November 2005, then in his fiftieth year of scale modeling; he related that he'd moved into a larger home and his layout had grown seven times in size. He added that he often invites 25 to 30 of his fellow modelers in to help run as many as 120 separate train sets at once.

Then there's Bruce W. Zaccagnino of Three Bridges, N.J. The ex-hobby shop owner modestly called his model railway layout "the world's largest." Zaccagnino may have a point: His layout contains 2.5 miles of track, over 1,000 switches, 400 bridges, and a whopping 37 tons of plastic rock. Devoting 14 to 15 hours at a stretch to his hobby, he once declared in a 1988 interview with Jim Doherty in *Smithsonian Magazine,* "I love it and I'll probably keep doing it until the day I die. Michelangelo never finished with his art and I won't either."

The Science Museum at South Kensington in England displays a miniature locomotive, the *New Castle*, that actually predates any full-size engine of its kind in the world. British inventor Richard Trevithick created the train in 1797 as one of the succession of experimental designs that later became the historic engine that ran from Camborne in Cornwall on Christmas Eve, 1801.

Whistles were installed on engines in Great Britain as early as 1833. The story may be apocryphal, but supposedly their use was inspired by a collision between a George Stephenson Samson steam engine and a market cart laden with egg cartons and butter. Distraught by all the scrambled egg on the track, the manager of the Leicester and Swannington R.R. came up with the idea of a trumpet-shaped whistle blown by steam to alert other travelers of oncoming trains.

The Maharajah of Gwalior in central India once had an indoor railway that served his guests at the dining table. The electric train ran along the table top with a load of exotic wines and aperitifs. Whenever a guest lifted his chosen libation from the coach, the train remained stationary until the bottle was replaced. Locomotive, coaches, and track were of solid silver.

Then there's that memorable television skit from the 1950s pulled off by Jackie Gleason that involved a toy Lionel train that ran on a bar carrying a beverage. Gleason, wearing top hat and tails in the role of rich-boy tippler Reggie Van Gleason, pushed a button, the train whistled and smoked as it delivered the shot glass, then went chugging on its way. Gleason pretended to grimace as he realized it was real scotch, and the audience roared when he ad-libbed the punch line, "Booze is swell with Lionel." Joshua Cowen, who was pretty straitlaced, was outraged at first, but then the Lionel skit made headlines and his buddies congratulated him, for pulling off one heck of a plug. Cowen grudgingly conceded, "That was pretty good."

This writer fondly recalls a time in the 1980s when his young son Josh actually looked forward to visits to the pediatrician. The allure of this particular doctor's office in the small town of Peterborough, New Hampshire, was a Lehmann Gross Bahn train set which whistled and chugged away on a supended overhead track and circled the waiting room.

Military hospitals in World War II and the Korean War were known to use elaborate toy train layouts as diversion and therapy for disturbed veterans.

A trendy move in the 1950s was the addition of train sets in fast-food chains and coffee shops across the land to travel up and down lunch counters and deliver hamburgers and ice cream sodas to the customer, then put it in reverse to return to the kitchen.

Toy trains were also known to have been placed in the harems of rajas and sultans, as a means of easing the boredom of the concubines.

Arthur Raphael, one of Joshua Cowen's early sales managers, was fond of writing imaginary dialogues between salesman and buyer. Raphael authored a children's book, *The Great Jug*, in 1936, about a brother and sister who are transported by giant bird to a magic forest where toy trains grow on a big tree. It was no coincidence that the toy trains pictured dangling on the limbs were Lionel *Hiawatha*-type steam engines.

The fascination and lore of trains is clearly enriched in the storytelling tradition in children's books, adult fiction and mysteries with a drum roll of distinguished authors—Frank Norris, Zane Gray, Rudyard Kipling, Hugh Walpole, Agatha Christie, and W.H. Auden and his classic poem, "Night Mail":

Pulling up Beattock, a steady climb—
The gradient's against her but she's on time.
Past cotton grass and moorland border,
Shoveling white steam over her shoulder.

Immensely popular children's fare such as *The Little Engine That Could* by Watty Pippin (1930), *Polar Express* by Chris Van Allsburg (1986), and *The Little Train* by Lois Lenski (1940) have all been rushed back into print recently. The Van Allsburg classic came out as a movie in the fall of 2005, starring Tom Hanks, and Lionel issued a *Polar Express* special commemorative train set featuring a big die-cast No. EB53 Berkshire steam locomotive with puffing smoke, a tender, and two lighted coach cars, along with tiny articulated characters from the film.

More recently, a number of highly recommended children's books with trains in the forefront appeared almost simultaneously: *I Dream of Trains* by Angela Johnson, *All Aboard* by Mary Lynn Roy, *Prairie Train* by Marsha Wilson Chall, and *The Train They Call The City of New Orleans* by Steve Goodman. Critic Tony Hiss in the *New York Times Book Review* characterized them as "tales that weave in and out of a dreamlike world of first journeys and longed-for leavings, while also relying on the familiar icons of brave engineers, lonesome whistles, and songs that sink deep inside you and won't let go."

When Joshua Cowen died of a stroke on September 8, 1965, the New York Times obituary stated that he had made the Lionel name "the third wing of Christmas among with the evergreen tree and Santa Claus." Certainly Cowen, more than anyone in the hobby, succeeded in conjuring up the tableau of running the toy train under the tree, accompanied by shrieks of joy from tiny tots—a family tradition played out in homes across the land. It may well be the first and most memorable association most of us have with toy trains.

Commodore Matthew Perry, when he first visited Japan in 1852, carried with him a letter from President Millard Fillmore suggesting the country would benefit by opening up trade with the West. It was a time when isolationist Japan distrusted all foreigners and certain noblemen wanted any intruders found within their borders to be executed. Perry also made another significant presentation: a gift of a miniature railroad set together with a lineside telegraph. Mesmerized by a tiny train speeding by at 20 miles per hour, the Emperor was also astonished that the telegraph "spoke" Japanese as fluently as English or German. It's uncertain whether Perry's ice-breakers had an important bearing on the subsequent treaty which was heralded as bringing Japan into the modern world. The gift undoubtedly helped thaw out diplomatic tensions. Ironically toys, including toy trains, soon becoming one of Japan's best-known exports, returning the favor so to speak.

Clarke Durham is well known for creating the spectacular CitiBank Station, in NYC, a hugely successful month-long Christmastime toy train display with magnificant dioramas that recapture the allure of real life railroading over the past 60 years. The striking 32-foot-high Victorian structure attracted over 125,000 visitors a few years ago. Durham, a veteran theatrical designer of such Broadway hits as *Brown Sugar* and *The Me Nobody Knows*, once remarked that he found scale modeling an avenue of self-expression, but he also enjoyed running his trains. He asked, "Why can't I be 10 years old once in a while if I feel like it?"

The late John Allen of Monterey, California, a professional photographer and one of the most visible pioneer modelers, was known as "the Great Pooh-Bah." He delighted in inviting friends to his home to help him operate, under rigid railroading procedures, his line, Gorre & Daphetid (pronounced "gory and defeated") which took him 20 years to build. Occasionally Allen, a practical joker, was known to hide a laugh box under the layout to "spook" his pals at critical intervals. Once he secretly mounted magnets inside two freight cars, making it impossible for his befuddled cohorts to couple them.

Milton Bradley, one of the foremost makers of lithograph paper-on-wood toy trains in the 1860s–1900s, supposedly got his inspiration for marketing illustrated toys and games after being assigned a design project for a special railroad car for the Pasha of Egypt in 1856. Even though untrained in that field, Bradley had been hired by the Wason Car Mfg. Co. in Springfield, Massachusetts, which manufactured real-life locomotives and passenger cars. Bradley's design was so well received that he was awarded a colored lithograph of the completed car.

The usually astute Louis Marx rarely made a marketing blunder, but his 1930s *Animal Express* was a humdinger. Marx felt that a whimsical little glass-eyed tin rabbit figural windup locomotive, with chicks and ducklings lithographed on hopper cars filled with jelly beans, would be a big seller for the Easter season. Marx failed to allot enough time to the new set for the short spring season, and the rabbit "died." Louis Marx later growled that he never wanted to hear about it again, ever. Were he alive today, Marx might feel some vindication in the knowledge that the surviving bunny trains bring big money and are hotly pursued by collectors.

The Lionel "Dummy" crane car from the early 1900s that recently brought an exorbitant $46,200 at auction is very primitive in design, and supposedly was one of a group assembled by founder Joshua Lionel Cowen himself in a small workshop from 1900 to 1905.

Joshua Lionel Cowen, like another famous curmudgeon, W.C. Fields, had an uneasy truce with the toddler set. In introducing a host of postwar railside accessories including automated cars, bridges, tunnels, and power stations, he explained that youngsters soon tired of simply running their trains in circles. "A few minutes of that and the little nippers will wander off and squeeze out some toothpaste or set fire to the curtains. They've got to get in on the action."

Don Fernandez, in "Trains: Railroading for Grown-up Boys" in the *Time-Life Encyclopedia of Collectibles*, tells this story about noted train devotee and author Ron Hollander, who once paid a visit to ex-Brooklyn Dodger catcher and Hall-of-Famer Roy Campanella, intending to interview him for a book. Hollander discovered that Campanella, a paraplegic as a result of a car accident a few years earlier, had turned to toy railroading as a diversion and owned a vast trove of 150 trains and accessories. Hollander was particularly interested in two highly desirable postwar Lionel steam locomotives, the #773 *Hudson* and the #746 Norfolk & Western. He subsequently closed a deal with Cam-

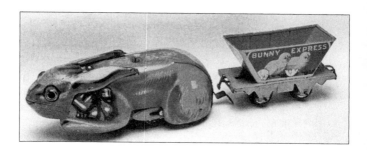

panella for the entire collection and added, "It was a special thrill to get the trains of one of my boyhood baseball heroes."

The record price for a toy train set may be the $200,000 tag (excluding delivery and installation) for an RMI Railworks Grand Empire Railroad riding-scale loco that runs on propane, and has two gondolas, a banquet, and a stock car for backyard travel. This precision replica is featured in the 2005 Neiman Marcus Christmas catalog.

Marx Animal Express, boxed; Bunny locomotive w/ 7 gondolas, 1936: $4,410—New England Toy Exchange Sale, 2004.

Collector from the Far Right

Conservative political pundit George Will discoursed some 30 years ago on the subject of toy train loyalties, of all things. Will, who makes no secret that he's in the American Flyer camp, issued this tongue-in-cheek statement: "On one side were loutish children who preferred Lionel trains (Lionel tracks had—and still may have, for all I know—three rails for Pete's sake). On the other side were precocious and discerning children who rejoiced in American Flyers, like my model of a Pennsylvania Railroad steam locomotive. I believe then, and still do, that children who embraced Lionels had dark pasts and dangerous futures." George Will's reaction upon later hearing the news that A.C. Gilbert had sold out his American Flyer interests to Lionel is not a matter of record.

Four Great Collections for the Ages

There are any number of high-profile collector/dealers in the hobby. One of the names that crops up repeatedly is Ed Prenderville of New Vernon, New Jersey, who may well own, on balance, the preeminent collection. Tom Sage of Allentown, Pennsylvania, a dealer/collector of European and American trains, has brokered deals for numerous world class collections over the past 40 years. In Europe, David Pressland of Maidstone, Kent, England, an avid train collector, also authors books on vintage tinplate toys and penny toys. Another prominent European collector is Gilles Herve of France. Then, of course, there's the following foursome, whose legacies have been dispersed in recent high-voltage auctions.

Barrett's Kimball Collection Parts I and II

Ward Kimball, a two-time Academy Award–winning Disney animator and producer-director, who created Jiminy Cricket and humanized the modern Mickey Mouse, shared with his wife Betty a love of scale model trains. Ward Kimball's first purchase was $400 for a real-life steam locomotive he rescued on its way to a Japanese scrap yard.

The San Gabriel, California, native loved to share railroad lore with another rail devotee, his boss Walt Disney. Kimball would fire up his functional live-steam rider locomotive, the *Chloe,* in his backyard, a three-acre orange grove, and head for an 1855 train station, on the property. The depot, which Kimball called *Grizzley Flats,* had originally been sited at the Pottsville branch of the Lehigh Valley Line, then later brought to the studio lot to make an appearance in the 1949 Disney film *Dear to My Heart;* Walt Disney later presented it to the delighted Kimballs.

When Ward Kimball passed away in 2002, the entire contents of the "Ward's Wonderland" collection were auctioned off at Noel Barrett's in two sessions at the Philadelphia Airport Ramada, Part I in November 2004 and Part II in May 2005. The combined auctions set a slew of records; the total blew past all estimates and set an all-time auction high for toy train collections at $5 million.

At Barrett's Kimball I Sale, the catalog cover showpiece was a ¾-scale model 706 B&O 4-4-0 locomotive and tender presentation award. Ward Kimball had added it to his collection for $125, just prior to

Legendary collector Ward Kimball with *Chloe,* his beloved steam locomotive, plus a few of his favorite toy trains.

Märklin Oriental Circus, 1900; cumulative total: $99,900 at Barrett's Kimball Sale, 2004.

World War II. The model's maker, Samuel M. Wilson, had worked in the master mechanic's office of the B&O during the 706 locomotive's heyday. Wilson's son sold it to get money to build two rabbit hutches. The B&O scale model highballed well past its estimates to $41,800.

Noel Barrett pointed out that "Kimball bought European trains when a lot of collectors weren't paying much attention to them. As a result he was able to amass an amazing collection when rare European trains were still available."

The story goes that the record setting $99,900 Märklin Oriental Circus Train Set sold at Barrett's in 2004 was purchased by Ward Kimball at a garage sale, for the princely sum of $500. The engine/tender, Menagerie Goods Wagon, Van Goods Wagon, and Oriental Circus Gas Wagon each went back to the

Continent; four separate lots sold to four different buyers. In battle of wills, an American and a German bidder pushed a 1909 Märklin Central Station with attached etched glass train shed to a rousing all-time high, $110,100. (The American buyer who won it indicated he was determined not to let the big station leave the country.) A new high was also established for a Märklin #2609 locomotive and tender colossus at $82,500.

Other Kimball sale individual records and highlights appear in our chapters Market Overview and Portfolio of Blue Ribbon Classics.

Poch Collections I and II

The Gerald Poch Collection, Parts I and II, sold at Bertoia's in 1999 and 2000, will be forever remembered for its incredible diversity and magnitude. When Bertoia's crew rounded up the collection at Jerry Poch's Connecticut home, they filled two 26-foot U-haul trucks, one with train sets and accessories, the other with no less than 10,000 original train boxes. The massive undertaking required nearly a week to accomplish. Bertoia kept three different experts busy cataloging the collection, one for Lionels, one for American Flyers, and one for European and other vintage trains. One or another specialist would exclaim, "There are only two known in this color," or "I only know of three of these." Any number of variants were previously uncataloged. Fellow TCA members attending the sale later conjectured that with a collection of this magnitude and quality, Poch's decision to divest had to be a case of collector burnout.

Jerry Poch, a successful entrepreneur has bought and sold a number of high-tech businesses over the years, netting him profits that were nothing short of incredible. At night, after a rigorous routine of running several companies, Poch would trade in his CEO's hat for a train conductor's cap. Jerry Poch recalled that he first began collecting trains in 1980 when he had a "little time between companies."

Catherine Saunders Watson quotes Poch in *Antique Toy World:* "My connection to toy trains, however,

Märklin #2609 locomotive & tender, early 1900s: $82,500

Märklin Central Station, with attached etched glass train shed, 1909: $110,100.

goes back to my childhood and not being able to own the magnificent Lionel and American Flyer layouts I saw at some of my friend's homes or on display at G. Fox, which was the upscale department store in Hartford, where I grew up. I was not one of those fortunate children who got a grand train set for the holidays. My only recollection is of something quite modest, a simple oval track that sat on the floor between the twin beds in the bedroom I shared with my brother."

When he eventually made the plunge to toy trains around 1980, Poch went at it full-throttle, gathering as many books on the subject as he could find. Over the ensuing 20 years, Poch went after the best available, and at this, his final train stop, devotees on board at Bertoia's soon bid willy-nilly in Philly for his collection of 2,000-plus lots of top-shelf train sets and accessories. Rarities abounded and, in many cases, duplicates and even triplicates roused the crowd. In introducing the collection at the sale's onset, Bill Bertoia predicted, "You can throw estimates out the window."

Bertoia was right; the top 22 entries, selling for a least five figures, rolled up a stunning $474,220. The Poch I total reached $1.58 million; Poch II: $690,000; and the grand total, $2.27 million, was the high-water mark for a train auction prior to Barrett Kimball's recent blockbusters.

While it was predicted to be primarily a Lionel-American Flyer show, Ives entries captured three out of the top five places. An Ives 1930 Circus Set with No. 1134 locomotive streaked to $71,500, a new record at auction at the time. A 1929 Ives Prosperity Special did justice to its name at $55,000; a Bing 1920s four-passenger set with Storkleg locomotive made $30,800; Ives ca. 1920 White Passenger set: $30,800; and the fifth was Ives again, with a unique 1931 O-gauge red Circus Train set at $27,500. The old adage that "cream rises to the top" rang true, as a single Ives Harmony Cream car, ca. 1922, rolled to $8,800, and a boxcar from the same dairy, ca. 1920, brought $6,600.

One dejected modeler aptly summed it up for his fellow underbidders in the hall when he yelled out after yet another astronomic raise from cyberspace, "You gotta be kidding!" Other highlights from Poch I and II appear in our Market Overview and Portfolio of Blue Ribbon Classics.

RM Auctions Kughn's Carail Collection Sales

Until recently, one of the most imposing private collections in the country was showcased in a remodeled bowling alley on Detroit's west side known as Carail. Proprietor Richard Kughn, a noted real estate developer and later CEO of Lionel, put a king's ransom's worth of vintage automobiles as well as thou-

Ives Wide-gauge Railway Circus set, w/ 1134 locomotive, 1930: $71,500—Bertoia's Poch Sale I, 1999.
Ives Harmony Dairy Cream tank car and boxcar, 1920s: $6,600.

sands of trains on display, including Lionel's coveted *Blue Comet,* American Flyer's *President's Special,* and an orange-and-black Ives beauty known as the *Pumpkin Set.*

Dick Kughn recalled that his first collecting venture entailed soap figures of Disney and Lone Ranger and Tonto characters. He gravitated to model trains nearly 70 years ago, when he was seven. Kughn was quoted in an interview with Tom McComas in *Toy Train Review On-Line,* "No other hobby does for a young person what model railroading does. . . . I learned about electricity, model making, designing buildings and train layouts—it was a tremendous learning experience. . . . Before I was ten years old, I studied about real railroads, about transportation."

Dick Kughn and his wife Linda elected to divest their Carail holdings several years ago, and the series of auctions has brought blockbuster prices. His two-day sale in September of 2003 grossed $4.6 million, and that's just part of a succession of sales intended to

Morton Converse Broadway-Lexington Trolley, lithographed tin, early 1900s: $1,540—Bertoia's Kuehnle Sale, 2005.

pare down the Kughns' holdings to a manageable size. It was no contest as to Carail's tour de force in the 24-hour marathon—a stunning 1,000-square-foot train layout featuring 12 bridges, and 11 Standard- and O-gauge trains. The layout, which took two artisans over a year to construct, raised the roof at a rollicking $218,500. An entire production run of Lionels (averaging 200 sets) from the year 2000 brought a bargain $19,950; the 2001 run: $29,325; the 2002 run: $12,075.

Other Carail auction highlights appear in Portfolio of Blue Ribbon Trains and Marketing Overview chapters.

Bertoia's Bernard Kuehnle Toy Feast Sale— Nov. 2005

The life-long train collection of the late Bernard Kuehnle of Toledo, Ohio, another giant in the hobby, was sold in a 400-lot segment of Bertoia's A Toy Feast Sale in Vineland, New Jersey, in November 2005. Kuehnle, a founding TCA member who had rarely missed a convention since 1968, was in his mid-90s when he passed away in 2005. The major thrust of his 50-plus-year collection was early Ives and American Flyer, in O and Wide gauge. Choice pieces included not one, but two rarely seen American Flyer *King George* V locomotives. Surprisingly they came in well under estimates at $2,750 and $3,575 apiece. Seldom seen Ives I-gauge inboard sets with original boxes proved the rule, rather than the exception. Many entries were gleaned from such

J. Butcher America scale model steam locomotive & tender display piece, 1890: $12,100— Bertoia's Kuehnle Sale, 2005.

Ives Grand Central Station, lithograph tin, 1930s— $2,475 Bertoia's Kuehnle Sale.

prestigious collections as those of Bill Clapper and William Ogden Coleman. Kuehnle was known to be painstaking in his research and religiously consulted original catalogs. His willingness to share knowledge and time with his colleagues was legendary. Kuehnle contributed input and loaned many of his prize Ives entries to be illustrated in *Greenberg's Guide to Ives Trains 1901–1932.*

Other Kuehnle highlights appear in Portfolio of Blue Ribbon Trains and Marketing Overview chapters.

Manufacturers and Distributors

Althof Bergmann, New York, N.Y.

1867–1880

Founders: Three Bergmann brothers, NYC jobbers, with J. Althof, another distributor

Specialty: One of the first U.S. toy distributors to market carpet-runner tinplate clockwork trains as well as horse-drawn toys, painted tin clockwork figures, acting primarily as distributors. In 1874 the firm secured several patents, one for a bell toy with three soldiers, and branched out as assemblers and makers of a large line of toys including doll-house furniture, kitchen stoves, banks, and bell and hoop toys.

American Flyer, Chicago, Ill.

1907–1966

Founder: John Hafner

Specialty: From the 1920s through the mid-1950s, AF's astute marketing strategy and vastly improved quality and performance standards made them a worthy competitor to Lionel in dominating the hobby on these shores. The AF line is distinguished by intricately detailed passenger and freight cars. Leading wide gauge sets include: President's Special from 1926; the Statesman, 1928–30; the Bluebird, 1927; the Pennsylvania R.R. K-5; the Hudson from the 1930s; the Burlington Zephyr, 1934–38; and Union Pacific City of Denver, 1936–39. Their HO line, introduced in the A.C. Gilbert era in 1938, are exemplified by the Northern Pacific and FY&P Passenger Sets. All of the firm's HO sets are highly prized by collectors.

Timeline:

1907—AF produced locos patterned closely after Ives' cast-iron steam outline 0-4-0s, but priced at considerably less.

1910—Originally known as Chicago Flyer, first reference to American Flyer Mfg. appeared in annual catalog; toy trains emerged as strongest line.

1914—Hafner left the firm in hands of W.O. Coleman, brought in as partner to oversee train line.

1916–1926—Marketed cast-iron clockwork trains under name Hummer I, II, and III, competing head-on with Bing and Ives in the U.S. market.

1918—AF introduced its first electric trains, converted Hummers.

1925—AF entered Standard gauge market, purchasing passenger coaches from Lionel, dressed them in their own livery.

1928–1930—Ives, now under receivership, was placed in joint control of AF and Lionel.

1938—A.C. Gilbert, known for boxed magic sets and Erector Sets, acquires a struggling AF, retaining only the name.

1929–1939—AF evolved from steam outline locos with cast–iron boilers with little attention to scale, to models with die-cast boilers, much closer adherence to scale, far greater detail.

1938–1963—American Flyer HO gauge, one of many designations given Gilbert Tru-Model Trains, heavy die-cast models offered in ready-to-run and kit form from 1938 to 1963, beginning with a New York Central–style Alco J3a 4-6-4 steam locomotive that enjoyed a 20-year run of popularity.

1948—No. 775 Talking Station made debut; called out train stops and other info.

1950—AF's 50th anniversary year, introduced Circus Set with red streamliner No. 353, plus two flatcars with cages and circus-type Pullman; Set included wild animal and performer cutouts and circus tickets.

(Greenberg Publishing has reproduced scarce original accessories.)

1951—AF introduced electronic air chime whistle which became standard on the No. 295 Pacific, 325 AC Hudson and the Sante Fe Diesels.

1955—A.C. Gilbert turned production over to Gordon Varney, who completely revamped the HO line that was basically rolling stock, but also featured an EMD F-3 diesel set. Varney also soon added a superb Northern Pacific passenger set.

1956—Entire toy train industry was in sharp decline, and after a decade of record sales, AF sustained heavy losses. Lower-priced HO gauge train sets soon glutted the market.

1957—Gilbert again took over production and switched from three-digit to five-digit identification system for HO- and S-gauge sets. Sleek and dashing diesels, such as the Alco DL-600, came to the fore in the late 1950s as well as a die-cast industrial switcher and revitalized Hudson locos. The five-digit versions had an all too brief production run and are much harder to find today.

1959—Gilbert contracted with Mantua-Tyco to turn out an HO (also sold in an S-gauge) rendering of an old time classic, the classic FY&P Passenger set, since acknowledged as the American Flyer's premier entry in HO gauge.

1961—A.C. Gilbert, having financial woes of it own, was acquired by the Wrather Corp., and its headquarters moved from Chicago to New Haven, Connecticut Introduced Pikemaster track, an S-gauge plastic track with closely spaced ties used to enhance appearance.

1963—AF abandoned HO gauge for two-railed system called S gauge. Distance between wheels reduced to 24 mm (⅞ in.) 1:64 scale, smaller than even the O gauge 1:43 scale.

1966—Wrather made drastic cutbacks, and though sales took a brief upturn, it was offset by borrowed capital and steep production costs. The firm officially closed its doors in 1966. Wrather sold its AF inventory to long-time rival, Lionel.

American Miniature Railway Co., Bridgeport, Conn.
1907–1912
Founders: ex-Ives, Blakeslee employees
Specialty: Turned out near clones of Ives gauge-O locos. Firm was on shaky financial footing and meager production runs did them in after five years,

American National Co., Toledo, Ohio
Early 1900s
Founders: Walter, Harry, and William Diemer
Slogan: "Raise the Kids on wheels"
Trade Name: "Giant"
Specialty: A.N. produced sidewalk playthings including scooters and bicycles; pressed-steel trucks, cars, and trains; and pedal cars competing with Keystone and Buddy "L" in the late 1920s.

Arcade Mfg. Co., Freeport, Ill.
1868–1946
Slogan: "They Look Real," adopted in 1920 Founders: E.H. Munn and Charles Morgan
Specialty: Originally known as Novelty Iron Works; E.H. Munn, one of the firm's officers, began turning out toy coffee mills in 1884 when name was changed to Arcade. Original specialty had been plows, harrows, and water pumps, and full-size coffee mills. In 1921 Arcade signed a licensing agreement with Yellow Cab Co. in Chicago to produce replicas of their checker cabs. Arcade was soon shipping out several thousand a day. Added a full line of farm and utility toys, Ford Model A's and T's, and Mack trucks. Turned out a number of cast-iron locomotives and train sets, including a cast-iron Pullman Railplane No. 3800X in the mid-1930s.

Arnold Co., Nuremberg, Germany
1906 to present
Founder: K. Arnold
Specialty: Stationary seam accessories, nautical toys; introduced Rapido gauge-N model railroads in 1960s.

Atlas O, LLC, Hillside, N.J.
1924 to present
Founder: Stephen Schaffan Sr.; later joined by his son Stephen Jr.
Specialty: Originated as a general machine shop. The Schaffans embarked on model railroading line in 1949. Over the years, Steve Sr. patented such innovations as Super-Flex track, Snap-switches, and custom line turnouts. Atlas's extensive line includes HO- and N-gauge locos, including 25

different freight car types in over 265 paint schemes. Web site: www.atlasrr.com

Bachmann Industries Inc., **Philadelphia, Pa.**
Maker of realistic HO-scale 4-6-0 steam locomotives and accessories in a line known as Spectrum. A recent edition, a loco and tender, is patterned after catalog standard steam Compound design by Baldwin, an early nineteenth-century maker. Web site: www.bachmanntrains.com

Bassett-Locke, **Northhampton, England**
1899 to present
Founder: Wenman J. Bassett-Locke
Specialty: First distributor to recognize and market leading German train makers as suppliers in Great Britain, including Bing, Carette, and Issmayer. Bassett-Locke commissioned British outline train beginning in 1900. When Georges Carette retired to Paris in 1917, Carette's dies were acquired by Winteringham, a British firm, which assumed the manufacturing for Bassett-Locke; Carette legacies were found in B.L.'s catalog as late as 1940.

Eugene Beggs, **Patterson, N.J.**
1872–early 1900s
Founder: Eugene Beggs
Specialty: Produced well-designed toy American outline steam locomotives in 4-4-4 configuration. Included were such embellishments as nickel-plated fittings and cut-glass headlights. The Beggs name symbolized the very best in available U.S. steam trains for some 30 years.

Biaggi, **Rome, Italy**
1946 to present day
Specialty: Beginning in the mid-1940s, this small firm turned out almost hand-built, limited runs of top-shelf, expensive toy trains, primarily locos in gauges O and I as well as small units of rolling stock. Biaggi locos such as the Sakai (1947) and Etat Mountain (1955) bore a remarkable resemblance in size and design to those of Märklin, just prior to World War II.

Gebrüder Bing, **Nuremberg, Germany**
1866–1933
Founders: Brothers Ignatius and Adolph Bing
Specialty: Wide range of steam, clockwork, and electric trains, as well as autos, boats, and other transportation toys. By 1882, Bing was exporting their line of trains to the U.S., Great Britain, and France. Bing's triumphs were many, including the ca-1900 Black Prince series of 4-4-0 steam locomotives in the four largest gauges and the L.N.W.R. *Precurser*, ca. 1905, created as a scale model for Bassett-Locke. Some of Bing's low-end sets were probably made by Iss-

mayer. Bing closed its doors during the Depression in 1933. Karl Bub acquired the train division and J. Fleishmann, the nautical toys.

R. Bliss Mfg. Co, Pawtucket, R.I.

1832–1914: Sold to Mason & Parker, Winchendon, Mass.
Founder: Rufus Bliss
Specialty: A major developer and early leader in lithographed paper-on-wood toys including trains, horse-drawn rigs, boats, building blocks, and doll houses.

George Borgfeldt & Co., New York, N.Y.

1881–1962
Founders: George Borgfeldt, Marcell and Joseph Kahle
Specialty: By the early 1900s, Borgfeldt, formerly a partner in a major toy firm in Austria, Strasburg's Pfeiffer & Co., emigrated to NYC where he opened a sample house of toys. Customers placed orders and items were drop-shipped from various factories. By 1920 he represented over 250 manufacturers. Borgfeldt, in the late 1920s and 1930s, marketed German comic windups under the name Nifty, such as the Toonerville Trolley and Oh Boy pressed-steel trucks, cars, and trains.

Boucher, New York, N.Y.

Early 1920s–1934: Bought out Voltamp.
Specialty: Boucher changed Voltamp's line to Standard gauge, but faithfully adhered to large well established lines, except for a Blue Comet 4-6-4. In 1929, Boucher opted out of trains and returned to its original pursuit of producing model boats; closed its doors in 1934.

Bowman Co., Norwich, England

1920s–unknown
Specialty: Produced rugged, oversized steam-powered O-gauge locos swith large boilers, closer to gauge I in scale. Passenger coaches ran a full 17 in., longer than most gauge-I coaches. Freight cars were crude wood affairs. Hand-decorated goods wagons are especially scarce and sought after.

Milton Bradley, East Longmeadow and Springfield, Mass.

1861 to present
Founder: Milton Bradley; James Shea Sr. took over firm after Bradley's death in 1911, but retained company name.
Specialty: Milton Bradley's first job, ironically, was as draftsman who designed a locomotive for Wason Car Mfg., which manufactured real-life railroad engines and cars. Later, after branching out on his own, Bradley became renowned for board games, blocks, books, educational games, and lithographed paper-on-wood toy trains and

rigs. Bradley acquired McLoughlin Bros. in 1920. Hasbro Industries bought out Bradley in 1984. Logos at various stages identified firm as Bradley Co., Milton Bradley & Co., and Milton Bradley Co.

George Brown & Co., Forestville, Conn.

1856–1880

Founders: George Brown and Chauncey Goodrich.

Specialty: George Brown was the first toy maker to use clockwork mechanisms; also the first to produce clockwork tin trains, beginning in 1856. Merged with J.&E. Stevens in 1868; the firm became the largest and most revered makers of mechanical and still banks; also produced cast-iron bell toys.

Karl Bub, Nuremberg, Germany

1851–1966

Founder: Karl Bub

Specialty: Bub's forte was handsomely enameled and later lithographed clockwork tinplate transportation toys, notably trains. F.A.O. Schwartz, of NYC, distributed Bub trains during the 1920s and 1930s. Bub acquired Bing's train division in 1933. Bub trains were targeted to the low-end market and tended to be less exciting than Bing or Märklin. Decorative boxes tended to portray dramatic if naive railway art which promised more than it delivered inside. Bub's factory was bombed several times during World War II. As the last surviving old Nuremberger, Bub risked all of its postwar capital in the new S-gauge system, which proved a disaster. They struggled on with a few gauge-O sets, before ceasing production entirely in 1966.

Buddy "L," Salem, Mass.

1910 to present

Founder: Fred Lundahl

Specialty: Underwent numerous corporate name changes, beginning with Moline Pressed Steel (1910–1913); Buddy "L" Line was introduced in 1921 and embraced brawny, oversized pressed-steel buses, trucks, and construction and utility toys as well as trains. Line was named after Lindahl's son Buddy. The widely popular Buddy "L" Outdoor Train Sets and their Industrial Set, introduced in 1920, flourished into the early 1930s. These were rugged toys that youngsters actually rode around the family backyards and are highly prized by collectors today. (See Market Overview chapter.)

Georges Carette, Nuremberg, Germany

1886–1917

Founder: Georges Carette

Specialty: Carette, a Frenchman, migrated to Nuremberg in 1886, and with Gebrüder Bing's financial backing, tinplate clockwork luxury limos and salon cars, boats, and trains; some were enameled, but most were lithographed. Carette was esteemed for top-quality, nicely detailed electric trams and model train sets. The firm featured an electric streetcar running on track at the 1893 World's Columbian Exposition in Chicago. One of Carette's scarcest and most desirable entries, the 1909 S.E.C.R. rail coach and motor coach, in steam or electric, is superbly lithographed in the livery of the Southeastern and Chatham Railway in both gauges O and I. Carette was deported from Germany in 1917 and his firm confiscated by the government. Carette parts and dies, acquired by a small British jobber, were reincarnated in trains marketed by Bassett-Locke.

Carlisle & Finch, Cincinnati, Ohio

1895–1915 (Toys) Still operating today with line of marine searchlights.
Founders: Robert S. Finch and Morton Carlisle
Specialty: Not a mainstream train maker initially, C&F produced a line of electrical novelties, dynamos, motors, gas engines, battery-operated electric railways, trolleys, trains, and accessories, including stations with automatic signals. The first successful manufacturer of electric toy trains in the U.S., C&F introduced a four-wheeled electric tram in 1897 and eight-wheel inter-urban in 1898. Later, they expanded line to include steam outline locos and rolling stock. Also served as a distributor, handling Knapp Electric's first toy automobile in 1900. C&F dropped its toy train line at onset of World War I to produce marine lighting for the military. Throughout their production-run history, not a single piece of equipment bore the C&F name. Railroad names, numbers, and design characteristics were sole means of identifying the Cincinnati firm. The list of heralds they used is brief but helpful: Lake Shore & Michigan Southern Railway (L.S. & M.S.R.); Hocking Valley (H.V.); B&O Railroad (B&O R.R.); New York Central & Hudson River (N.Y.C. & H.R.); Pennsylvania Rail Road (P.R.R.); (the following could be one of three) Newton & Monroe, Newton & Marion, or Newark & Mansfield (N. & M.)

Dayton Friction Toy Works, Dayton, Ohio

1898–1935
Founder: David P. Clark
Specialty: Sheet-steel friction flywheel-powered novelty transportation toys, including trolleys and trains under name "Hill Climbers." Clark marketed friction cars and trains with patented flywheel under the name "Gyro." Produced pressed-steel child riding toys up to 24 inches long under name Son-NY.

Clyde Model Stockyards, Glasgow, Scotland

1789

Specialty: Early maker of brass steam-powered locos; also brokered trains by Radiguet et Massiot, and Bing entries such as the Black Prince series.

Morton E. Converse, Winchendon, Mass.

1878–1934 (Mason & Converse until 1883)

Founder: Morton Converse

Specialty: Converse's Toytown Complex was once hailed as largest wood toy factory in the world; Converse produced lithographed paper-on-wood as well as metal transportation toys including floor-running trolleys. Made the first trolley bodies for Lionel in 1902, including the classic *City Hall Park*.

Corcoran Mfg. Co., Washington, In.

1920–1940

Specialty: Oversize pressed steel riding toy autos and trains under names "Cor-Cor."

Corgi Toys, Mettoy, Swansea, South Wales

1956 to present; originated as Playcraft Toys. Merged with Mettoy Playfield, Ltd., in 1956.

Specialty: Toy vehicles in 1/45 to 1/48 scale, including trains in cast metal and plastic.

Denton Hardware, Fullerton, Pa.

1895–1937 (Continued as a cold storage hardware manufacturer until 1973.)

Founders: Henry H. Dent and four partners

Specialty: Cast-iron and aluminum transportation toys and banks, introduced in the 1920s with only moderate success. Dent is known for intricately cast, realistic high stack cast-iron locos and train sets, as well as Mack trucks; also the comic *Toonerville Trolley* and a cast-iron version of the *Amos 'n' Andy Fresh Air Taxi*.

Doll et Cie, Nuremberg, Germany

1868–1946

Founders: Peter Doll and J. Sondheim

Specialty: Low-end steam engines and accessories; novelty train and cars in steam; also fanciful enameled clockwork carousels, Ferris wheels, and other amusement park rides and attractions.

Dorfan Co., Newark, N.J.

1924–1933

Founder: Joseph Kraus

Specialty: Kraus, who started the firm under the name Fandor/Kraus in his native Nuremberg, emigrated to the U.S.

in 1923 and renamed it Dorfan (or "Fandor" syllables reversed). Dorfan produced its first electric train in 1925, the Electric Constructive Locomotive; they also marketed the first train construction set in the hobby. By 1926, Dorfan locomotives propelled their way to the top in operating performance. However, their pressure die-castings, whose precision enabled the bodies of locomotives to do double duty as frames for the motors, had a fatal flaw. Lightweight and unbreakable when new, castings all too soon suffered metal fatigue. In the late 1920s, the New Jersey firm added a small line of appealing O-gauge train sets to their distinctive tall, art-deco-styled Standard-gauge locomotives. Collectors clamored for the DO loco 0-4-0, in orange with green roofs, brass trim, and Pleasant View Pullmans in 1928; the red No. 3920 and green or red No. 3930 Loco-Builder engines in 1930. The Depression and failure to keep up to speed and mass-produce with the giants, American Flyer and Lionel, led to their demise. Production ceased in 1933, but a sizeable inventory kept Dorfan in the action until 1938. Loyal Dorfan collectors place the firm in the U.S. top four (dethroning Marx).

Dorfan Firsts:

- Die-cast loco bodies
- Readily assembled loco construction kit
- Switchboards, aka panel boards
- Drive wheels and axles removable as single unit
- Inserted (separate) window frames in passenger cars
- One unit detachable drive wheels and axles
- Die cast passenger car wheels
- Ball-bearing locos
- Remote controlled train stop signals
- Directional remote control for locos
- Remote control uncoupler

Dowst (U.S.) "Tootsietoy," Chicago, Ill.
1876 to present
Founders: Charles & Samuel Dowst
Specialty: Miniature cast-metal transportation toys, primarily autos. Brand name Tootsietoy was in honor of a Dowst granddaughter, Tootsie. Produced its first train set in 1921.

Elektoy, Harrison, N.J.

1911–1913
Founder: J.K. Osborn
Specialty: Elektoy produced a surprisingly large number of detailed stamped metal I-gauge trains over a brief span of only two years, prior to World War I. Elektoy lacked national distribution, being confined to small hardware store and electrical supply houses. They also suffered from poorly designed hook-slot couplers.

J. Falk, Nuremberg, Germany

1898–1940
Founder: J. Falk
Specialty: Stationary steam engines, optical projectors, steam-propelled boats and trains. Inexpensive but imaginative.

James Fallows & Sons, Philadelphia, Pa.

1874–late 1890s
Founder: James Fallows
Specialty: This firm was a continuation of Francis Field Francis, of which Fallows was head designer and inventor; it first bore his name in 1880. By 1894 it traded under name Frederick & Henry Fallows Toys, producing painted and stenciled tinplate horse-drawn rigs, boats, and trains. One of the few early makers to identify their product, Fallows used "IXL," a bit of wordplay meaning "I excel," on their products. The advent of lithographed tin toys in the 1880 contributed to Fallows' demise.

H. Fischer, Nuremberg, Germany

1901–early 1930s
Founder: H. Fischer
Specialty: This low-profile toy marketer issued comic/character toys under the Nifty trademark which were primarily jobbed out in the U.S. by George Borgfeldt. Also carried line of tinplate clockwork toys and trains with their own logo, a fish swimming through the letter A. (Not to be confused with Georg Fischer, a Nuremberg maker of penny toys.)

Fisher-Price Toys, East Aurora, N.Y.

1930 to present
Founders: Herman Guy Fisher, Irving L. Price, and Helen Schelle
Specialty: Lithographed paper-on-wood and plastic pull toys, featuring scores of whimsical Disney comic/characters and Mother Goose figures. Fisher-Price was bought out by Quaker Oats in the early 1970s and is now a subsidiary of Mattel. Train-related favorites include: *Pushy Pat Engine* (1933); *Streamline Express No. 215* riding toy (1935); *Teddy Choo-Choo* (1937); *Mickey Mouse Choo-Choo* (1938); *Tabby Ding-Dong* (1939); *Peter Bunny Engine No. 321* (1941); *Donald Choo-Choo* (1942); *Golden Gulch Express* (1961).

Gebrüder Fleischmann, Nuremberg, Germany

1887 to present
Founder: J. Fleischmann
Specialty: Quality tinplate boats, automobiles, trains. Fleischmann acquired Doll et Cie just prior to World War II. The firm specializes in model railroads to this day.

Francis Field & Francis, Philadelphia, Pa.

1838–1870
Founders: Henry and Thomas Francis
Specialty: A predecessor to Fallows, FF&F produced line of tinplate clockwork toys and trains which went by name of Philadelphia Tin Toys in the late 1840s. James Fallows joined the firm in 1870 and by 1880 had assumed ownership.

Fulgerex (originally Elettren), Lucerne, Switzerland

1947 to the present.
Specialty: Elettren, an Italian train maker, made only two locos: an Italian Steam Outline *Pacific* and a 4-4-4 electric, available with one or two motors; both of these 1950 entries were larger than normal O gauge. Elaborately detailed, they rate among some of the finest ever produced. The firm was later acquired by Count Giansanti Coluzzi, a noted collector of cars and trains in his own right and renamed Fulgerex.

Garton Toy Co., Sheboygan, Wis.

1879–1976
Founder: E. Bassingdale Garton
Specialty: Cradles, toy carts, wagons, velocipedes, and pedal cars and locomotives.

Gendron Co., North Toledo, Ohio

1872 to present
Founder: Peter Gendron
Specialty: A Canadian, Peter Gendron invented a process for manufacturing spoked wire wheels, and started his wheel goods company marketing baby carriages and velocipedes. Merged with American National Corp. in 1927, although Peter Gendron spun off his own firm as Gendron Wheel Co. By 1990 Gendron produced a full line of wheeled child's toys, plus wicker furniture and bicycles, under the trademark Pioneer. Acquired by the Howe Company in 1964. Gendron's most successful years were the 1920s when the Pioneer Line was world-renowned.

Gibbs Mfg., Canton, Ohio

1884 to the present
Founder: Lewis E. Gibbs
Specialty: Gibbs initially made plows. Beginning in 1886, Gibbs introduced toys, specializing in key-wind and string-

pulled spinning tops. The firm added children's wagons and lithograph paper-on-wood, tinplate, and advertising toys.

A.W. Gamage, London, England
1890s–late 1920s
Founder: A. W. Gamage
Specialty: Gamage, a leading London emporium, also ran a successful mail-order toy outlet throughout Great Britain. Gamage placed large orders abroad with Bing, Märklin, Carette, and Issmayer. By 1906, a majority of trains in their catalog, numbering over 150 different models, were British outline entries, mostly exclusive to Gamage. Primary suppliers for the English trade were Bing, which concentrated on the most impressive top-shelf lines, while Märklin supplied lower quality sets known for ungainly, chunky styling—completely the opposite of their roles on the American scene. Two typical Gamage locos of the period were the Bing 4-4-0 *Black Prince* and Märklin's British experimental O-gauge 0-4-0 decapod clockwork version. Gamage's status in the toy train market dwindled dramatically in the 1920s.

J. Garlick Co., Patterson, N.J.
1888–1890s
Founder: Jehu Garlick
Specialty: Garlick was a small manufacturer of quality steam toys and I-gauge trains. Prior to 1888, Garlick marketed steam trains in association with Eugene Beggs. A patented reversing valve attached to the cylinder distinguishes most early Garlick locomotives.

Gendron Wheel Co., Toledo, Ohio
1872 to present
Founder: Peter Gendron
Slogan: "Line that sets the pace"
Specialty: Produced wheel chairs tricycles and pedal cars. Merged with American National Corp. in 1927 and was acquired by the Howe Co. in 1964. Now part of Cons Co., maker of hospital equipment.

A.C. Gilbert, New Haven, Conn.
1908–1966
Founder: Albert C. Gilbert
Specialty: Gilbert made boxed magic sets, and his ingenious Erector Sets, introduced in 1913, were an instant hit, with 30 million sold over the next 40 years. Gilbert bought out Richter Anchor Blocks and an American affiliate, Mecanno, in 1914. Pressed-steel toy autos and trucks were also added in 1914, plus a variety of scientific toys. Gilbert acquired American Flyer in 1938 and moved it into his New Haven headquarters, after the premier train maker encountered fi-

nancial woes. Gilbert later would suffer financial losses of its own and sold its AF toy inventory to Lionel in 1966.

Girard Mfg. Co., Girard, Pa.
1908–1966
Also traded as The Toy Works (1919–1922) and Girard Model Works, Inc. (1922–1935)
Founder: Frank E. Wood.
Slogan: "Making Children Happier"
Specialty: Girard produced toys and trains bearing the Marx label under a commission sales agreement in the early 1920s. Girard also traded under their own label, Woods Mechanical Toys. Lines are distinguishable only by name. The firm turned out electric trains beginning in 1927–1928. The first set from the soon to be famous Joy Line was a No. 350 loco with matching cars; this particular line was a popular seller into the mid-1930s. Girard, after a split with Louis Marx, went into bankruptcy in 1934, although toy production struggled on until 1975. In 1972, Quaker Oats bought out Marx's interest in Girard as part of the Marx U.S. and Great Britain Toy Division.

S.G. Gunthermann, Nuremberg, Germany
1877–1965
Founder: Sigfried Gunthermann
Slogan: "The world is my field!"
Specialty: Sigfried Gunthermann ran the company until his death in 1890. His widow married Adolph Weigel and toys from 1890 to 1919 bore a maker's mark with shield inside a circle with his initials, A.S.G.W. Tinplate clockwork renderings of autos, whimsical clowns, and other comic/character figurals are highly collectible, although paint flaking is a common flaw with this imaginative toy maker. Gunthermann built and then exported American outline 4-4-0 locos with prominent cowcatchers. The firm's production was disrupted for the duration when its Nuremberg factory was bombed out early in World War II. Gunthermann was acquired by Siemens in 1965.

Hafner Mfg., Chicago, Ill.
1900–1950
Founder: W.F. Hafner
Specialty: Originally known as the Toy Auto Co., Hafner merged with Edmunds-Metzel Co. in 1907 to manufacture trains and mechanical autos. Name was changed to American Flyer Mfg. in 1910, but Hafner embarked on his own in 1914, and was joined by his son under the name Hafner Mfg. Co. For the next 35 years Hafner manufactured inexpensive windup trains. Firm was sold to Wyandotte in 1950

and when that toy maker went out of business, Marx acquired Hafner's dies.

Harris Toy Co., Toledo, Ohio
1887–1913
Specialty: Harris made cast-iron wheel toys—horse-drawn rigs, autos, and trains; also filled out its catalog with unbranded merchandise supplied by Dent Hardware, Hubley, and Wilkins. Harris sold its assets to a metal tubing fabricator following financial difficulties.

M. & J.L. Hess, Nuremberg, Germany
1826–mid-1930s
Founder: Mathias Hess
Specialty: The founder and later his son John Leonard Hess, who took over after the elder's death in 1886, produced tinplate pull-along trains and various other parlor toys. Hess also produced penny toys, notably trains. Friction-powered autos bore the Hessmobile trademark. Hess and Issmayer led the way in developing strong miniature clockwork mechanisms for locomotives as early as the 1870s.

Hornby, Liverpool, England
1920s to present day.
Slogans: "Long Running—Strong Pulling"
"Mechanics Made Easy" (referring to its Meccano line)
"Every Boy Chief Engineer of His Own Railway"
Founder: Frank Hornby
Specialty: Hornby produced Meccano toy trains beginning in the 1920s, with Märklin as licensing agent in Germany. Surprisingly, little effort was made to penetrate the lucrative U.S. market. Märklin supplied Hornby with steam engines and other accessories. Used a number of different logos to distinguish various lines: Dublo, Tri-ang (merged with Hornby in 1947), Hornby Railways. Hornby's elaborate embossed gilt lettered leather-like boxes and colorful annual catalog, the *Hornby Book of Trains* (first appearing in 1920), proved infinitely more impressive that its actual train sets. Hornby tried construction kits with little success and dabbled with a line of more conventional Nuremberg-style tab and slot train sets, in brightly colored heavy enamel. The firm's late 1920s electric O-gauge Metropolitan Railway locomotive set, made lavish use of lithography. A huge double-track Hornby engine shed may be the finest lithographed building made by any toy maker prior to World War II. Its French outline *Nord* 4-6-2 *Pacific* loco, reduced to a 4-4-2 with two coaches, became Hornby's most popular large locomotive. Hornby continues today to produce toy trains and slot cars under the name Hornby Hobbies, now manufactured in the Republic of China.
Web site: hornbyhobbies.com

Howard Electric Novelty Co., New York, N.Y.

1900s–1910

Specialty: This rather obscure maker, along with Carlisle & Finch, was one of the leaders in making lightweight electrical-powered steam outline trains in II-gauge, beginning in 1904. Ungainly and of questionable quality, Howard did offer working headlights. Its one standout, a No. 8 loco 999, an elegant 4-4-0 entry bearing the New York Central Line livery, was not enough to keep them afloat, and they ceased operation in 1910.

Hubley Mfg. Co., Lancaster, Penn.

1894 to present.
Founder: John E. Hubley
Slogan: "They're Different"
Specialty: Originally Hubley produced cast-iron electric train equipment and parts. Hubley's finest cast-iron motor toy was the *Double Track Elevated Railway*, patented in 1893. Also noted for high-end horse-drawn rigs such as two-, three-, and four-seated brakes, and carriages. Cast-iron toy autos, cap guns, trucks, banks, and doorstops became Hubley headliners in the late 1920s and early 1930s. Hubley surmounted Depression woes with a low-budget line of toys. Iron shortages and military contracts in World War II led to Hubley's disbanding its toy division in 1942. Later, Hubley's inventory was acquired by Gabriel Industries, a division of CBS.

Hull & Stafford, Clinton, Conn.

1860s–1880s (Est. as Hull & Wright; acquired Union Mfg. in 1869)
Specialty: Enameled clockwork tin toys, including trains, boats.

Issmayer, Nuremberg, Germany

1861–1930s
Founder: Johann Andreas Issmayer
Specialty: In the 1880s Issmayer produced lithographed tin American outline trains, mostly of the less expensive novelty type. Small 30 mm gauge (not quite O gauge) and I gauge were Issmayer specialties by the early 1900s. Issmayer sets are seldom identified by the firm's name, but an often-used winged wheel logo is a telltale clue. Issmayer was one of the true precursors of classic lithograph tin penny toys. Issmayer also supplied the entire Carette line of clockwork trains and several Schonner and Bing gauge O and smaller clockwork 0-2-2 sets during this period. One of the finest Issmayer sets, the Pacific Express (I gauge, 1895) was made for the U.S. market. Issmayer, like Bub and Kraus, was never really visible in the peak years and, after a

shakeout among German makers, finally disappeared from the scene in the early 1930s.

Ives, Blakeslee & Co., Bridgeport, Conn.
1872–1932
Founders: Edward R. Ives and Cornelius Blakeslee
Slogan: "Ives Toys Make Happy Boys"
Specialty: Ives founded E.R. Ives & Co., in Plymouth, Conn., in 1868; they originally made baskets and hot-air toys. Most Ives early trains were initialed "I.M.C." (Ives Mfg. Co.). Ives made clockwork toys and trains in tin and cast-iron (later die-cast metal). Ives continued to market clockwork trains long after it entered the electric train field in 1910.

Timeline:

1874—Edward Ives invented a painted tinplate loco, the Whistler, that featured an air whistle and became a staple in his burgeoning toy line.

1880s—Ives, one of the earliest makers to recognize catalogs as a pivotal marketing tool, issued two a season, running to several hundred pages.

Mid-1890s—Ives became the first U.S. maker to produce clockwork trains that ran on tracks, a common practice with the Germans beginning in 1880.

1904—Ives turned to lithography to embellish its locos. The firm produced almost identical copies of Märklin and Issmayer sets in European I gauge, keeping the gauge active in the line into 1920.

1901–1910—Ives, spearheading large cast-iron locomotives, became the Nuremberg makers' most intense competition.

1909—Innovated a wrap-around catalog, directing their sales pitch to 12-year-old boys.

1909—Ives introduced its popular Miniature Railway System, with clockwork loco and Twentieth Century Limited passenger cars.

1910—Edward Ives, though reluctant to make the transition, was eventually persuaded by his son Harry to add electric-drive locos to their line, patterned after New York Central's S-class electrics.

1912—The firm added the Observation, the most atypical, widely copied of all passenger coaches, to its gauge-I range. The coaches featured unique and decorative open end platforms. Sold as a single train, the Observation surprisingly wasn't included in Ives O-gauge sets until 1923.

1920s—Ives' major technical coup, a patented three-position automatic-sequence reverse, was the envy of its rivals AF and Lionel.

1921—Ives abandoned I gauge in favor of Wide gauge (2¼ in. between rails), their version of Lionel's Standard gauge. The new sets, a cut above Lionel styling, were better proportioned and detailed down to the last rivet, but Ives incurred higher manufacturing costs to achieve it.

1925—Ives borrowed heavily to finance its transition from cast-iron to light, strong die-castings.

1928—Ives declared bankruptcy on the eve of one of its finest entries, ironically called the *Prosperity Special*.

1928–1930—Ives name continued under the joint control of Lionel and American Flyer who purchased their inventory.

1930–1932—In 1930, American Flyer relinquished their share in Ives to Lionel, who relocated the factory to Irvington, N.J. Ives name was carried by Lionel only into 1932. A few Ives-Lionel sets came out in 1933, only to see a complete name phase-out by the end of the year.

Summary

Ives and its predecessor Ives, Blakeslee is the most revered name in the toy world, particularly in the clockwork model genre. The name is consistent with quality. Ives cast-iron No. 3239 and No. 3240 series rank among the all-time I-gauge classics. Among the most coveted Ives entries were privately labeled specials with logos of various companies and mercantile outlets. Noteworthy are the *Pony Express* set, (Macy's?) John Wannamaker Nos. 3241, 3242, and 3243 locos in the department store's maroon colors; the F.A.O. Schwarz No. 3239 loco; Harmony Creamery flatcars. Most Ives sets had relatively brief production runs, and scarcity proved a deterrent over the years in attracting collectors. A fiercely loyal coterie of Ives devotees still exists, though not in the numbers that flock to American Flyer and Lionel.

Jouets en Paris (J.E.P.), Paris, France

Known originally as Societe Industrial de Ferblanteriel, name was mercifully changed to J.de.P. in 1928, then J.E.P. in 1932.

1899–1965

Specialty: Lithographed tin clockwork trains, autos, other transportation miniatures. After World War II, J.E.P. produced France's finest O-gauge trains, exemplified by the die-cast Mistral 12-wheel electric loco and P.L.M. 2-8-2 steam type with twin engines. J.E.P., after an abortive attempt to adopt the new HO system, closed its doors in 1965.

Kato USA, Schaumburg, Ill.

Dates and Founder: Unknown

Specialty: Kato currently makes precision scale-model trains in HO and N gauge.

Web site: www.kastousa.com

Keystone Mfg. Co., Boston, Mass.

1920s–date unknown

Specialty: Keystone's first major output was toy motion picture machines; later added pressed steel motor trucks, fire engines including Siren Riding Toys and Ride-Em Trains. In the post-World War II period, most of Keystone's output was leftover inventory from Kingsbury's defunct toy division.

Kilgore Mfg. Co., Westerville, Ohio

1920–1940s

Slogan: "Toys That Last"

Specialty: Kilgore purchased George D. Wanner Co., the largest U.S. maker of kites, in 1925. Main specialty was cast-iron cap guns, cannons, and paper caps. In 1928, they merged with Andes Foundry Co. and Federal Toy Co. to create America Toy Co., with cast-iron motor toys as a specialty. By the late 1930s, Kilgore concentrated mainly on cap pistols.

Kingsbury Mfg. Co., Keene, N.H.
(see also Wilkins Toy Co.)

1919–1942

Founder: Harry T. Kingsbury

Specialty: Originally know as the Triumph Wringer Co., Wilkins made washing machine wringers, but when their miniature salesman sample wringer became an instant best-seller, they chose to market it as a toy. Kingsbury bought out Wilkins in 1895 and combined with Clipper Machine Works, which specialized in mowers and reapers. Kingsbury introduced toy autos and trains in the early 1900s, faithfully copying real life prototypes. Harry Kingsbury's durable patented spring-steel sealed motor and hand-painted enamel finish proved major selling points. Wilkins' name was dropped following World War I. Kingsbury's toy line was discontinued in 1942 and its inventory was sold to Keystone.

Knapp Electric & Novelty Company, New York, N.Y.
1890–1913
Founder: Knapp (first name unknown)
Specialty: Knapp was one of the earliest U.S. manufacturers of wet cell–powered trains and other transportation toys. Knapp first produced 2-in. gauge electric locomotives in 1902 with Carlisle & Finch as its distributor. Knapp, continually beset by lack of cash flow, survived until 1913, done in by inability to create a strip track capable of withstanding its heavy cast-iron locomotives and rolling stock.

La Rapide, Paris, France
1920s–1954
Founder: Louis Rouissy
Slogan: "Fastest in the world"
Specialty: La Rapide produced electric and clockwork model trains, toy race cars, and oval tracks. In the 1930s, they excelled with smartly styled die-cast O-gauge trains, attributing their speed to their heft and low center of gravity.

Ernest Lehmann Co., Brandenberg, Germany
1881–1951 (when it was renamed Ernest Paul Lehmann Patentwerk)
Lehmann Gross Bahn, Nuremberg (train division)
1968 to present
Founder: Ernest Paul Lehmann
Specialty: Lehmann emerged as a leading manufacturer and world exporter of superbly lithographed and painted tin string-pull, leaf-spring, keywind, inertia, or flywheel powered toys from 1888 to 1929. In 1951, when its business was taken over by communist government of East Germany, Lehman was reestablished in Nuremberg under the name Ernst Paul Lehmann Patentwerk. Overseeing the firm were Wolfgang and Eberhard Richter, sons of Johannes Richter, heir to the original Lehmann enterprise, who died in 1956. In the mid-1950s Lehmann reluctantly produced its first plastic toys, and was quick to encounter cutthroat competition from cheap imports from Korea, Japan, Hong Kong, Signapore, and Taiwan. In 1968, the Richter brothers took a bold step in introducing Lehmann Big Train ("Gross Bahn" in German), a true-to-scale 45 mm gauge G in 1:22.5 scale. The LGB product line has seen an unprecedented international acceptance in recent years. The Lehmann G-gauge line today includes over 30 locos, 60 cars, and nearly 200

accessories. In 1989, Lehmann introduced a live steam locomotive which actually uses steam to power the model. Web site: grossbahnen.de

Linemar, Japan

1930s–1960s
Slogan: "Linemar, best by far"
Specialty: A Marx (U.S.) manufacturing subsidiary that marketed Disney, comic/character, and space toys, mostly battery operated.

Lionel Corp., New York, N.Y.

1900 to the present
Lionel Mfg. Co: 1900–1908; Lionel Trains Inc.; 1987 to present
Founder: Joshua Lionel Cowen
Slogans: "The Standard of the World" (Lionel Mfg., 1909)
"Trains to grow up with, not out of" (Fundimensions, 1980s)
Specialty: Lionel ranks as the preeminent name in U.S. model trains and is the sole survivor from the so-called U.S. Big Four.

Timeline:

1901—Lionel produced an ungainly looking battery-powered flatcar in 2⅞ in. gauge.

1902—Published its first catalog, a black-and-white edition featuring the celebrated City Hall Park Trolley.

1906—Introduced and copyrighted the innovative Standard-gauge line, carving its own special niche in the hobby. Also introduced three-rail track in its 1906 catalog.

1912—Lionel was able to achieve a highly competitive prices by using lustrous enamel finishes with rubber-stamped lettering and limited bright brass trim. Their 2⅛-in. track size gave the impression that Lionel trains were wider, taller, and brawnier than the gauge-I models by rivals Bing, Märklin, and Ives.

1915—Lionel added O gauge to its repertoire.

1917—Lionel introduced the first automatically controlled model train operation.

1918—Actual door panels and window inserts in locomotives for greater strength and realism. Another patented extra, etched brass plates, were affixed to locomotive bodies.

1922—Joshua Cowen established the Societa Mecca-nnica Le Precisa in Naples, Italy, for experimenting, researching, and testing Lionel models and tools.

1923—Added as Lionel accessories were miniature brick houses with dormers and sun porches. These included replicas of the childhood homes of Lionel vice president Mario Caruso and his inventor brother Louis in Irvington, N.J.

1924—Lionel added latch couplers to its O-gauge cars.

1925—The firm patented a die-cast wheel with nick-eled steel rim over tread to provide added reliabilty and improved performance. Insulated fiber frogs (junction between two arms of a turnout or points, grooved for wheel flanges) were added to Lionel switches. Further improvements included headlights with individual switches and red and green transpar-ent side panels.

1926—Lionel scooped the industry with remote-control switches, though the non-derailing feature did not debut until 1931.

1928—Lionel is first to introduce remote control elec-trically operated couplers. Also introduced Build-a-Loco kits to compete with A.C. Gilbert's Erector sets.

1930s—Lionel introduced the State Set with 408E loco; Illinois, Colorado, California, and New York par-lor cars; working lights, swiveling armchairs, double washrooms with miniature hinged toilet seats, and revolving chairs—the most elaborate mass-produced toy train set ever.

1933—Lionel introduced the Chugger, a device that imitated sound of a steam-driven loco.

1934—At the height of the Depression, with Lionel in temporary receivership, Cowan initiated the Mickey & Minnie Mouse handcar, pumping up the volume to over a quarter million units in one year. The real re-versal of fortune, however, came when Lionel acted quickly as the first to cash in on the advent of real-life streamliners. Exemplified by such Lionel interpreta-tions as *City of Portland* diesel, Union Pacific *City of*

Denver and *Flying Yankee,* all in O-gauge, 1/45 scale, Lionel enjoyed its best pre-Christmas sales in history.

1935—Lionel introduced a locomotive whistle powered by DC current. The whistle was operated by a separate controller and sounded remarkably authentic.

1930–1942—Lionel's "golden years." Mammoth steamers, splendid terminals, bridges, tunnels, power stations, and other railside paraphernalia, as well as sleek torpedoes, including the *Hiawatha* and *Zephyr* in O gauge. The trend toward realism peaked in the scale model *Hudson.*

1942—Lionel suspended toy train production for the war and turned out navigational equipment for the U.S. Navy.

1944—Due to shortage of metal, Lionel issued a paper Wartime Freight Train to keep its name before its customers. This boxed set, with 250 intricate cardboard pieces with slots and tabs, was marked "ready to assemble," but proved to be a nightmare for many a dad who attempted to fold and piece the set together.

1946—A new Penn. R.R. 20-wheel S-2 steam turbine became a Lionel mainstay in post–World War II years. The firm also introduced white smoke pellets and "choo-choo" sounds (probably creating the greatest impact of all its accessories), electronic controls, a water tower, and realistic freight cars.

1948—Lionel added a popular battery-powered diesel horn.

1950—Union Pacific streamliner and Fast Freight debuted. Lionel introduced "Magne-traction" (wheels and axles were magnetized for greater traction and pulling power).

1957—Lionel belatedly introduced HO trains; too late to help flagging sales.

1958—Lionel sales dipped 23 percent to $14.4 million, its first red-ink year since the Depression.

1959—Lionel's publicity campaign introduced tiny operable helicopters launched from flatcars. *Life* magazine photographers were on hand at Newark College gymnasium to capture 400 Lionel flatcar helicopters taking to the air en masse.

1959—In a hostile takeover, a group led by attorney Roy Cohn, former chief counsel on the Alger Hiss case, purchased Lionel from Joshua Cowen and his daughter Isabel. Joshua's son Lawrence, president of the firm, was left out of the loop. Cohn, who took over the troubled firm, could not stem the losses and subsequently bailed out. An investment group acquired it, but they, too, severed ties before the year ended.

1960—Army missile specialist Gen. John Medaris became Lionel's president. New sets featured rocket launchers and other weaponry as accessories. Made of plastic, they were flimsy and tended to break easily; they did not appeal to adult railroaders.

1969—Ronald Saypol, a Cowen relative, took command, but Lionel was soon derailed and out of the train business.

1970–1980—After having been bought out by General Mills, the firm was renamed Fundimension and headquartered in Mt. Clemens, Mich. New trains were the GP-7 and GP-9 diesels bearing over 20 different railway names. Fundimension also added HO trains from 1974 to 1977, with indifferent results. New models were issued only sporadically, and trains and accessories reappeared in ensuing catalogs only if inventory was left over. Lionel was essentially reduced to a tiny loss-making subsidiary of a giant conglomerate.

Early 1980s—Fundimension moved its manufacturing facilities to Mexico. Many feel that their train sets and accessories from 1982 and 1983 lacked the quality of the glory years.

1985—Kenner Toys acquired Lionel from Quaker Oats. Kenner focused on direct-marketing to consumers, with little success.

1986—Richard Kughn, a real estate developer and toy train devotee in his own right, purchased the firm, now known as Lionel Trains, Inc. (LTI). Kughn soon accommodated die-hard Lionel fans with a formidable lineup including Reading T-1, Rock Island Northern, and particularly Texas & Pacific-type locomotives.

1995—Kughn sold LTI to Wellspring Associates LLC, a Manhattan-based investment broker with musician Neil Young as partner. LLC since appears to be coping well in a highly volatile but still viable market. The group recently introduced a Transmitter Command Control (TMCC), an electronic system for O-gauge three-rail model and toy trains which permits operation of multiple trains on the same track, without complex wiring; also give locomotives digitized sounds. TMCC has since been licensed to be compatible with non-TMCC trains as well. Web site: Lioneltrains.com

Other Lionel Firsts

- Automatic block signals
- Automatic warning signals
- All steel electrically lit miniature villas and bungalows
- Roller contact shoes on locos
- Automatic crossing gates
- Three-bearing armature shafts on miniature motors
- All steel locos and car bodies
- Trucks with nickeled journals
- Reinforced phosphor-bronze wheel axle bearings; armature shaft

Lutz, Nuremberg, Germany
1850s–1891
Specialty: One of the earliest purveyors of luxury enameled-tin clockwork and steam-driven floor trains. The celebrated Queen Victorian Royal set from 1875 is attributed to Lutz as well as a classy 4-4-0 American outline loco. Lutz, known for detailed, precise handwork in its sets, lacked the knack of volume production, and formed a perfect synergy when incorporated with the fast-rising Märklin in 1891, marking the dawn of a new era of German toy trains.

Gebrüder Märklin, Göppingen, Germany
1859 to present
Founders: Theodor and Caroline Märklin. Founder's sons took over firm in 1888 and name changed to Gebrüder (Brothers) Märklin.
Specialty: Märklin originally made doll-size tinplate kitchenware. It soon expanded its line to enameled tinplate boats,

aeronautical toys, autos, and trains. The firm is unsurpassed in production of clockwork, steam, and electric train sets. Märklin was the first to envision train sets as part of an entire miniature railway system including stations, rail-side equipment, scenery, and even toy passengers and engineers. In the post–World War II era, Märklin became sole survivor among early German makers. The firm made giant strides as a viable train marketer, and its miniature N-gauge trains rate high praise among collectors.

Timeline:

1920s—Märklin gets a second head of steam after troubled war years. They add a series of fine electrics to their growing stable of Reichbahn steam outline locos.

1930s—Introduced the articulated Swiss *Crocodile* in gauge I as well as O, ca. 1933.

1935—As part of its O-gauge international collection, Märklin added a NYC Central *Hudson; Commodore Vanderbilt*; an uncataloged earlier Hudson model; L.N.E.R. *Cock o' the North* (G.B.); and Borsig, 4-6-2 *Pacific* (Ger.). Märklin reduced the scale to gauge OO, half the size of O and later called HO. The sets were of matchless quality and looked amazingly realistic. By the late 1930s, they were marketed as precision scale models and compared to exquisite Swiss watches.

1951—Much to the chagrin of Märklin loyalists, it turned to injection-molded plastics for its locomotives, retaining metal frame.

1958—Firm produced an ingenious Telex coupler permitting operators to remotely uncouple locomotives anywhere on the layout without special uncoupling track; introduced freight car kits the same year.

1963—A milestone year in which Märklin produced its one-millionth No. 3000, a model of an early British outline classic, the BR89.

1969—Märklin introduced an economy line called Primex for department stores and smaller outlets; a popular entry was the No. 3193 class 01 *Pacific*. Firm also introduced a more realistic appearing K-track in which running rail was roll-formed from stainless steel strips, which had special appeal to modelers. Later L-track continued with stainless steel, but added molded plastic ties.

1979—Märklin unveiled a fully digital model railroad at the 1979 Nuremberg Toy Fair and marketed it beginning in 1984.

1984—Märklin celebrated 125th anniversary with a gift set, No. 3300, a metal edition of the Swiss *Crocodile;* and the E194 known as the German *Crocodile;* also a BR44, 2-10-0 steamer reissue.

Today—Märklin remains an major global force in the hobby with a full range of HO, Z, and MAXI/I-gauge trains. Web site: www.marklin.com

Louis Marx & Co., New York, N.Y.
1919–1979
Founders: Louis and David Marx
Slogans: "Quality is not negotiable"
'"One of many Marx toys, have you all of them?"
Specialty: Louis Marx, who had worked with toy firms Ferdinand Strauss and C.G. Wood, began his own operations with a commission sales agreement for toys made by these firms as well as trains from Girard Model Works—all sold under the Marx trademark. Marx worked his magic with two defunct Strauss toys, *Zippo Climbing Monkey* and *Alabama Minstrel Dancer*, selling $8 million dollars worth over the next two years. Marx purchased molds from Strauss in 1927 and began producing his own trains.

Timeline:

1927—Marx introduced Joy Line 350 lithographed tin clockwork trains and continued to offer them in its catalog until the mid-1930s.

1928—While other toy makers were struggling to keep afloat at the advent of the Depression, Marx revived an age-old toy, the yo-yo, and reportedly sold over 100 million.

Mid-1930s—Began manufacturing clockwork and battery-operated tin comic/character toys through its Japanese subsidiary, Linemar.

1932—The third major edition of the successful Joy Line engine in red and black stamped steel.

1935—Marx acquired Girard and renamed it Girard Mfg. Co. producing pressed-steel autos and trucks, as well as a popular line of 6-in.-long tin lithographed trains. Girard went to a heavier stamped steel frame for both its clockwork and electric Joy Line sets.

1936—The first Marx train set after acquiring Girard, the *Commodore Vanderbilt* locomotive with 6-inch cars in various colors, was launched. This entry would be a staple in the line into the 1970s.

1930s to 1941—Marx's finest era. They produced lithographed tinplate four-wheel and eight-wheel models in a variety of colors. Perhaps Marx's most detailed and desirable sets were the No. 500 *Army Supply Train* and articulated streamliners, led by the MX No. 732 Union Pacific diesel. To enhance play value, Marx began practice of including both freight and passenger cars in a single set.

1940s—Just prior to World War II, Marx added a line of realistic 3⁄16-in.-scale freight cars, competing head on with American Flyer. The firm was kept busy with military contracts through most of the decade; by 1950 it made a smooth transition back to toys and trains, producing over 12 percent of all toys manufactured in the U.S.

1948—Marx's first foray into hard-plastic train sets was a flop, as they were not durable enough for child's play; the firm soon switched to polyethylene.

1949—The No. 333 die-cast loco 4-6-2, one of the handsomest Marx ever produced, arrived to complement the 3⁄16-in.-scale passenger cars.

1950—An exciting new addition was the Sante Fe diesel set with two "A" unit engines, one powered, the other a dummy. This banner year also heralded the arrival of 7-inch tin trains personified by the No. 994 *Mickey Mouse Meteor Set*. Marx introduced a new automatic coupler in plastic for 3⁄16-in. rolling stock: a multi-directional scissoring attachment. Cars were disengaged by a projection in the track which tilted the couplers.

1955—Louis Marx was the first to be inducted into the Toy Hall of Fame. His plaque acclaimed "the Henry Ford of the toy industry."

1959—Marx took a step backward in history with the William Crooks loco, a realistic black plastic replica of a William Crooks prototype built by Smith & Jackson of Patterson, N.J., back in 1861.

1972—Marx's low-priced electric trains and clock-work windup toys failed to excite the new generation of collectors. In 1975 Marx sold its assets to Quaker Oats, who also owned Fisher-Price Toys and later, Lionel. Name was changed to Marx Toys. Quaker Oats, in less than a year, sold Marx at a loss to European toy maker Dunbee-Combex Marx Ltd. Most damaging was the firm's failure to cash in on the popularity of space toys and electronic games in the mid-1970s.

Marx used highly sucessful mass-production techiques and concentrated on major accounts with Sears and Woolworth's on the low-end market

1979—Marx division entered bankruptcy after Dunbee scrambled to liquidate extensive warehouse inventory via a series of blockbuster auctions in various cities. Included were boxed Marx examples plus those of Lehmann, Lionel, Chein, and other makers Louis Marx had accumulated. The auctions, though an unprecedented windfall for collectors, failed to raise the requisite funding to revive the ailing firm.

2000—The rights to Marx's toys and trains are now scattered among a number of companies, and some of its products are still being produced. Marx Trains, Inc., offers litho trains, K-Line makes O-scale train cars and scenery, and Model Power produces HO-scale trains from old Marx molds.

The firm's popularity in the hobby is undeniable, and the novelty trains they produced, as well as those by their Japanese Linemar affiliate, are avidly pursued by toy train and Disney collectors alike.

The Marx name has since changed hands on several occasions. Despite having similar names, neither of

Marx-branded firms of today have any connection to the original Louis Marx & Co. or Marx Trains, Inc.

Micro-Trains Line, Talent, Ore.
1980 to present
Specialty: Z- and N-gauge model trains
Web site: www.micro-trains.com

MTH, Columbia, Maryland
Owner: Mike Wolf
Specialty: MTH makes quality, nicely detailed O-gauge train sets. Its economy line is known as Rail King.
Web site: www.mthtrains.com

Overland Model Inc., Muncie, Ind.
1976 to present
President: Brian Marsh
Specialty: Importers of all-brass HO-, S-, and O-gauge limited-run scale model railway sets, made in Republic of China and Korea.
Web site: www.overlandmodels.com

Paya, Alicante, Spain
Early 1900s–1960s
Specialty: Paya made O-gauge clockwork trains beginning in 1918; added electric in 1927. Locomotives were primarily 4-4-4s; coaches were long, handsomely lithographed entries. Paya also added nicely lithographed toy autos, motorcycles, and aircraft, marketed in Spain and France.

Ernst Plank, Nuremberg, Germany
1866–1930s
Founder: Ernst Plank
Specialty: Prior to the 1890s, Plank made cabless steam powered "dribblers" for the British trade. Tinplate clockwork and parlor trains, airplanes, boats, and autos later became their strong suit. Typical of Plank's styling was the *Vulcan*, spidery with an upright cab, fashioned in brass or enameled tin. Outmoded recreations of ancient clunkers from the turn of the century managed to sustain Plank through the 1920s, but by the end of the decade, they had closed their doors.

Pratt & Letchworth, Buffalo, N.Y.
1880–1900
Founders: Pacal Pratt and William Letchworth
Specialty: P&L's forte was cast-iron floor trains, horse-drawn hansom cabs, and fire engines. They originally operated as Buffalo Malleable Iron Works. They acquired Carpenter's stock and patent rights in 1890 and introduced a full line of cast-iron horse-drawn rigs and motor powered vehicles.

One of the firm's most popular entries, the imposing ca. 1892 *Vestibule Train* (a.k.a. *Buffalo Express*), featured a No. 880 loco, tender, and two coaches, spanning 60 inches overall.

Pride Lines, Ltd., Lindenhurst, N.Y.

1980s to present
Specialty: Pride Lines made reproductions of the Walt Disney Collectors series of handcars popularized by Lionel, including Mickey and Minnie Mouse, and Donald Duck and Pluto. They also replicated numerous Märklin railside accessories such as street lamps and crossing signals.

Radiguet & Massiot, Paris, France

1872–1900
Founder: Radiguet; added Massiot as partner in 1899
Specialty: While its main focus was scientific and educational instruments, R&M was also one of the earliest train makers, producing brass steamers or "dribblers" in the early 1880s, with a certain panache typical of the French. Their locomotives were prominently featured in British train catalogs from 1880 to 1890. R&M also produced numerous parts for British toy train entrepreneurs.

Whitney S. Reed, Leominster, Mass.

1875–1897
Slogan: "Every Boy His Own Engineer"
Specialty: Lithographed paper-on-wood toys and construction sets, and building blocks. Reed's *Mother Goose* train set and *Reindeer Train* set represent the pinnacle in that genre.

Rico, Alicante, Spain

1930s–1950
Specialty: Produced low-end tinplate mechanical transportation toys, including trains under trademark RSA.

William Rissman , Nuremberg, Germany

1907–unknown
Founder: William Rissman
Specialty: Toy trains and mechanical motor toys.
Trade name Ri-Co is often confused with the Spanish firm. Usually, the word "Germany" following the name clarifies the toy as Rissman.

Rock & Graner Nachfolger, Nuremberg, Germany

1850–1904
Specialty: A small family firm that produced high-end parlor trains. R. & G.N. tried to emulate Märklin in producing quality clockwork tin trains and accessories in 1896. Outclassed as to diversity and lacking the capacity to compete

favorably with bigger German firms, R. & G.N. was liqui-
dated in 1904.

Charles Rossignol, Paris, France

1868–1962
Founder: Charles Rossignol
Specialty: Rossignol turned out quality enameled and lithographed clockwork vehicles including luxury cars and train
sets, almost exclusively for the French market. A fine specimen in detailing artistry, Rossignol's 1902 steam tram was
patterned after a little steamer prototype that ran through a
section of Paris. They added low-end electric trains to their
line in 1919. By the late 1950s, Rossignol's emphasis had
shifted almost exclusively to clockwork buses and autos.

Sakai, Tokyo, Japan

1930s to present
Specialty: In the 1930s, and then following World War II,
Sakai's staple—electric outline steam locomotives and
rolling stock—combined the best features of Märklin and
Lionel.

Schonner, Nuremberg, Germany

1875–1906
Specialty: This firm was one of the first German makers to
assimilate British steam technology, with cabless locomotive floor runners. A key Schonner design feature linked
working steam pipes from the steam dome to the cylinders.
For the next 20 years, they turned out rather ancient-
looking, elaborate steam locomotives in I, II, and III gauge,
readily identified by large pierced cowcatchers. Finally, in
1898, Schonner added clockwork locomotives. Their swan
song was a beauty—a wind-cutting Paris-Lyon-Mediterranee
RR *Coupe Vent* 4-4-0 steam outline loco, designed for the
French firm Heller & Cauday in 1906.

Jerome Secor Mfg., Bridgeport, Conn.

1872–1885
Founder: Jerome B. Secor
Specialty: Secor's original sphere was sewing machines and
caged singing bird toys. They produced the first cast-iron
clockwork loco in 1879, after the courts ruled in their favor
vs. Carpenter in a patent dispute. Secor was acquired by
Ives in the 1880s, but continued to design and manufacture
a variety of ethnic clockwork toys through Ives.

Stevens & Brown, New York, N.Y.

1869–1880
Founders: Elisha Stevens and George Brown
(see George Brown & Co.)

Stevens Model Dockyards, London, England

1843–ca. 1927

Specialty: This craft guild specialized in manufacturing and distributing toys and toy trains. Produced a number of sturdy steam-powered floor runners, including Thunderer and the largest British brass locomotive made, Greater Britain. Stevens passenger cars (or "wagons" as they were called) are scarce and seldom found intact. Stevens guaranteed in their 1926 catalog (their last) that every train featured was of their own manufacture. Though they made a least 15 designs of brass "dribblers," a number of German "sleepers" dominated the lineup.

Structo Mfg. Co., Freeport, Ill.

1908 to present

Founders: Louis & Edward Stohacker, C.C. Thompson

Slogan: "Structo Toys Make Men of Boys"

Specialty: Structo originally made Erector Construction Kits and, just after World War I, produced a line of eye-catching construction kits featuring stamped-steel push-pull transportation vehicles, including trains. Later, in 1928, when Gilbert acquired American Flyer, he then combined the firm with Structo. In 1935, the Strohacker brothers sold most of their assets to J.G. Gokey. With Gokey's passing, F. Ertel, a Dyersville, Iowa, farm toy maker, acquired Structo's patents and inventory in 1975, and continues to market the line.

Trix, Mangold Nuremberg, Germany

1927 to present

Founder: Stephen Bing

Specialty: Trix, better known in Great Britain as Trix Twin, produced reduced scale 1:90 German outline (and British outline when modified) electric trains in the same 16.5 mm gauge as Märklin. Though more expensive, of lesser quality, and more toylike than Märklin, the Trix system gained a foothold in Great Britain through Bassett-Locke. Stephen Bing fled to London to establish a factory for the British trade after his firm was taken over by the German government.

Unique Art Mfg., Newark, N.J.

1916–1952

Specialty: Comic/character tin mechanicals. Unique produced its first clockwork trains in 1949. Tried and failed to compete with Marx in lower-priced sets in the 1950s.

Voltamp Electric Mfg. Co., Baltimore, Md.

1879–early 1920s

Founder: Manes E. Fuld

Specialty: By 1903, Fuld designed an electric railway as a present for his son and soon Voltamp was marketing electric trains of the highest quality. Their 4-6-0 and 4-6-2 Pacific locos with eight-wheel tenders were acknowledged the finest produced by any maker prior to World War I. Aimed at the high-end market, Voltamp's production run was always limited. In the 1920s, Boucher, a leading maker of model boats, acquired Voltamp, continued with earlier tried-and-true designs and managed to attract a small, selective and highly affluent clientele.

Wallwork, Manchester, England
1890s–early 1900s
Specialty: The only British firm to produce cast-iron floor runner trains, a genre almost exclusively the domain of U.S. makers. Wallwork made only a few styles of locomotives, patterned after 1840 prototypes.

Weeden Mfg. Co., New Bedford, Mass.
1883–1939
Founder: William Weeden
Specialty: Weeden produced working toy steam engines as well as toy live steamboats, trains, and autos. Like its most exemplary toy steam, the tiny six-inch *Dart* (ca. 1888), their locomotives had such refinements as rivets on the boiler, embossed name plate, and realistic driving wheels. Weeden sold its assets to Pairpoint Co. in the 1930s.

Wells Brimtoy, Hollyhead, Wales, and London, England
1920 to present
Specialty: Wells made low-end tinplate autos and trains. They acquired the Brimtoy subsidiary in 1922. One of the many post–World War I British toy firms that appeared on the scene to help end the German monopoly on the Continent, Wells was perhaps best known for series of comic handcars from the 1950s featuring Cinderella, Mickey and Minnie, Donald Duck, and other Disney characters.

Wilkins Toy Co., Medford, Mass.
1890–1919
Founder: James S. Wilkins
Specialty: (See also Kingsbury) Wilkins served primarily as a broker of cast-iron autos and trains known for incredible standards of realism. Kingsbury bought out the firm and moved it to Keene, N.H., in 1895, but the Wilkins name continued on product lines up through 1919.

Williams Electric Trains, Columbia, Md.
1971 to present
Founder: Jerry Williams
Specialty: Williams turned out reproductions of vintage Lionel and Ives Standard–gauge trains. Williams had acquired

original tooling from the Lionel Corp. after it sold the rights to its name to General Mills in 1969. In the 1980s, Williams also obtained tooling that once belonged to Kusan, an obscure Lionel rival from the 1950s, and his product line switched to O gauge. Williams is known to add more details to its sets than were possible in the 1950s; they leaned toward a more traditional train, devoid of electronic gadgetry.

Web site: www.williamstrains.com ◼

4

MARKET OVERVIEW

Today, more than a half century since strip malls and suburban sprawl began to spread throughout America, the automobile and the airplane relentlessly have shunted trains into abandoned sidings.

But movement is afoot, roaring out of the roundhouse like the *Twentieth Century Limited*. It is the resurgence of accurately scaled miniature iron horses as collectors and modelers across the land conjure a dreamlike cosmos of first journeys and longed-for departures. All over the world, for this truly is the most universal of all collecting pursuits, miniature toy trains are chugging away from station to station and into the affections of the young and the restless.

The future for train collecting didn't appear all that rosy just a few years ago. First to sidetrack young armchair train engineers was the advent of television in the 1950s, with the average U.S. family riveted to their sets six hours a day, seven days a week. Then there were the tense, chaotic years following World War II, with the Cold War and threat of a nuclear disaster. The late 1950s and 1960s were also a time for relocation, and highly mobile families found less time to cart their train sets around with each transfer. Little League, Elvis, slot car racers, and foosball; an obsession with electronic games and action figures—all these distractions crowded toy trains off the schedule. Today, toy trains are going full steam ahead, and even if real-life trains disappeared altogether, most diehards, with their mania for miniaturized minutiae, would continue to pursue their quest.

An entire subculture of railroading enthusiasts has come of age. Its devotees range from traditionalists, often called rail fans, who still enjoy watching trains, both real life and replica; and retro-romanticists who acquire defunct railroad cars and locos and convert them to quaint homes or eateries; to authenticity-obsessed tinkerers known as scale modelers, who wouldn't dare trivialize their trains as toys and are known to devote years creating elaborate accurately scaled layouts. (Modelers may well comprise the largest contingent, an estimated 200,000 worldwide.) Armchair railroaders seem content to stay close to home and read about what the rest of the hobby is doing. Then there's the generalist, the devotee who pursues a broad spectrum of railroadiana—from ephemera to lanterns, signals, and other RR paraphernalia and engineer/conductor uniforms. The final category, perhaps the most high profile, is readily visible at antique auctions and shows—the pure toy train collector who concentrates on displaying entries in impeccable condition with original boxes. Each entry is treated with all the delicacy of a Fabergé egg. No putting trains through their paces on a track or layout here. The collector's focus may compel him to acquire complete sets by classic makers, or concentrate only on one type, be it locomotives (engines), trolley cars, or cabooses. Others collect by scale, period, medium (cast iron, copper tinplate, paper-on-wood), and motive power (push-pull, steam, clockwork, battery, electric).

The TCA is likely the largest of all collecting organizations with 31,500 members as of October 2005. Not far behind, the National Railroad Historical Society, founded in 1935, has over 22,000 members and 173 chapters in the U.S., Canada, and a number of affiliates overseas.

Harbingers of bullish times are the vast throngs who attend railroad swap meets all over the country. These include two "must be there" TCA events—one in April, the other in October in York, Pennsylvania—that draw over 10,000 devotees over a weekend.

Most modelers fit the profile of middle-aged, middle-class males. Collectors fall into the same gender and tend to be a little older. However, these are not the only train enthusiasts, and Lionel trains may present an example of a train manufacturer open to seeking out new markets. Lionel made a few half-hearted stabs at wooing the ladies that flopped: first in the 1930s when they produced a miniature electric range, and again in 1957 when they launched the ill-fated *Lady Lionel* set with a frosted pink engine and lilac hopper. On the rare occasions when they appeared in catalogs, the girl's role was that of an admiring sister posing in the background while her brother manned the controls. It was not until 1974 that Fundimensions, Lionel's new owner, launched an ad campaign with the headline, "Lionel trains: We never said they were only for boys." The campaign, praised by Ms. Magazine, was triggered by a letter Lionel received from seven-year-old New Yorker, Caroline Ranald: "Dear Sir. I don't like your ads. Girls like trains too. I like trains. I have seven locomotives."

There are two schools of thought as to what constitutes the golden era of electric trains. On one extreme the muscular Standard and Wide-gauge behemoths of the 1920s to 1930s beckon; on the other, the post-Depression smaller, less expensive, starkly realistic O-gauge models. Miniaturization made great strides in popularity as smaller trains took the hobby by storm in the post–World War II era. After the hobby went into a deep funk in the 1960s and 1970s with competition from video games and a new fad—slotcars—the 1980s saw a revival in larger-scale trains, although smaller scale kept its die-hard devotees. Harbingers of this large-scale renewal included the Lehman Gross Bahn's G scale, known as "Big Trains." There is also a lively market for over-sized classic sets from the 1920s and 1930s, such as American Flyer's *President's Special*, Ives' long cab *Olympian*, and Dorfan's *Champion Limited* in bright orange, propelled by a foot-long locomotive.

Although a large segment of collectors focuses on lo-comotives, a big market also exists for rolling stock, es-pecially cabooses and crane cars (e.g., Lionel No. 3360 *Burro*) or snow plows. Don Fernandez, in *Treasure Trains* (*Time-Life Encyclopedia of Collectibles*), points out that (a train's) age is not directly indicative of value; there are many more collectors out there who want a plastic engine such as the Lionel Great Northern No. 58 snow plow, which may be worth ten Bing cast-iron electric engines from the 1920s. Many collectors prefer to fill their sidings with unusual "off-beat" cars such as the 1960s Lionel *Bronx Zoo* livestock car with trick gi-raffe carrier, the Lionel No. 800 *Jail Car*, or a 1902 Märklin O- and I-gauge *Cistern Wagon*. Unaccountably, the color yellow as a paint scheme on any piece of rolling stock invariably commands a premium. A yel-low Märklin PRR No. 90309 caboose tooled to $7,700 in 2004; the red variant of the caboose would probably fetch about a third of that amount.

A superb passenger terminal or power station pro-vides a dramatic counterpoint to any realistic train layout. Collectors are known to have an adrenaline rush over star status examples: Witness the new world's record at-auction sale for the 1909 Märklin *Central Station*, sold at auction in May 2005 for a stunning $110,000. At the same sale, an Rock & Graner *Nachfolger* station shone at $71,500, an R&GN matching pedestrian footbridge with signals added $44,000, and an 1895 Märklin station topped off at $49,500—clear indications of collectors' will-ingness to pay top dollar for these accessories.

Electric trains tend to be less prone to cyclical value glitches than trains in tin, lithographed wood, cast

Buddy "L" Outdoor Train Set, pressed steel, 1921 (priced separately)—Barrett's Kimball Sale II, 2005.

iron, or other materials. One seldom sees dramatic upswings or prices bottoming out of electric trains at auctions or shows—though the Great Depression of the 1930s spelled dooms for a number of major train makers. Even trains that were failures when first introduced, such as Ives' *Prosperity Special* and Lionel's *Lady Lionel*, are fervently collected today, prized for their rarity. More post–World War II model electric trains command upper four- and five-figure prices today than any other contemporary toy genre; only a handful of 1950s robots and space toys have escalated in value over such a brief span. The new frontier or next level for collectors is postwar boxed sets in the best condition possible. These include the 1955 Lionel *Congressional* GG-1 electric and the 1963 Lionel *Space Prober* set with 6407 flatcar and missile or *Pencil Sharpener* Car. The Lionel *Father & Son* Set from 1960 (only three known) is so scarce that they seldom, if ever, appear on the market.

As demonstrated at Barrett's Kimball Sale II, crane cars, tankers, and cabooses rate highest among rolling stock categories.

"Lionel Trains Are Real Like Mine," counter display featuring roundhouse with five of Lionel's latest 1930s line of locomotives: $15,400.

Veteran auctioneer Ted Maurer staged his 35th Annual Thanksgiving Toy Train sale at the Ridge Fire Hall in Phoenixville, Pennsylvania, in November 2005. Highlights included the 30-year collection of lifelong TCA member Sam Lenhart, and prewar electric trolleys, postwar Lionel sets, and advertising promotional displays, and other toy train peripherals continued to dominate. A Converse No. 175 City Hall Park open trolley took off to $9,900; a boxed No. 100 closed-end trolley by an unknown maker and a dark green Rapid Transit Trolley each clanged to a rousing $11,500; and a No. 101 open-side Electric Transit Summer Trolley excelled at $9,350.

A Lionel 390E Blue Comet, enhanced by its original box, advanced to $5,830 while a Standard-gauge Baby State set, also boxed, sped to $5,060. Railside accessories loomed large: A Lionel No. 915 large, 60-inch-long tunnel made $1,265, while an Illuminated Terrace with tattered box lit up at $10,450. A Lionel industrial standup display from the early 1930s depicting a Power Station, Hellgate Bridge, and Engine House in its original mailing carton had the crowd aghast at a record $34,100. A three-foot-high die-cut counter dealer display of a railroad engineer tallied $15,400. Equally astounding, an Lionel Caboose Club pinback from 1918–1929 was no tail-ender at $880. A

Lionel promotional plant Air Raid Warden hard hat in flaming red made a scorching $825.

One of the most facinating outgrowth of the hobby is what is known as *garden-railroading*. Outdoor toy railroading has been with us for more than a century, particularly in Great Britain. It achieved a fair degree of popularity stateside in the 1920s and 1930s, but nearly faded from the scene following World War II. Its resurgence in the U.S. is at least partially attributed to the introduction of brawny, colorful LGB trains from Lehmann in Germany, beginning in the late 1960s. LGB has recently introduced more American-style train sets, and other large-scale train makers have chimed in as well. The "garden" part of the hobby also enjoys a growth spurt as women and children as well as men flock to their nearest nursery or landscaping center to acquire slow-growing bonzais and other dwarf and miniature versions of plants to fit the scale of the trains. The potential for using natural rock formations, ponds, and small streams on one's property makes for stunning vistas that surpass indoor layouts for sheer realism.

For further signs of a toy train renaissance, consider the unprecedented rush of watershed multimilliondollar estate auctions over the past five or six years.

The auction slate resonates with Bertoia's Jerry Poch Collection, Sales I and II, 2000–2001; Noel Barrett's Ward Kimball Collection I and II, 2004, 2005; Richard Kughn's Carail Collection, World Wide RM Group Auctions, 2003, 2004; Randy Inman's Richard Keats Collection 2000 and 2001; Lloyd Ralston's Dennis McDonough Collection, 1999; Ralston's Herb McBride Collection over years 1995–1999; Bertoia's Bernard Kuehnle Collection, 2005; and the Giansanti-Coluzzo Collection at various European and U.S. auction houses, the most recent at Lankes Auktionshaus, Döhlau, Germany in 2005.

As Ted Maurer summed it up: "If these trains don't quicken your pulse, dial 911." ◼

5

A PORTFOLIO OF BLUE RIBBON TRAIN SETS

The drum roll please—cue the music to Duke Ellington's "Take the A-Train." Behold the consensus Top 20 Blue Ribbon entries, selected on a highly informal, purely subjective basis by a number of movers and shakers in the hobby. We are certain that many of you could come up with still another twenty entries, and perhaps even twenty more random entries for an encore, that would prove every bit as desirable and representative as our picks.

1. Lionel Blue Comet, O-gauge with No. 400E locomotive, 1931–1934: $8,500—Bertoia Poch Sale, 1999.

2. Lionel Rail Chief Set, Hudson No. 700 & No. 793 combine locomotives, 1937: $4,125–Bertoia's Kuehnle Sale, 2005.

3. American Flyer *Hiawatha* O-Gauge Passenger Set, 1936: $2,090—Bertoia's Kuehnle Sale, 2005.

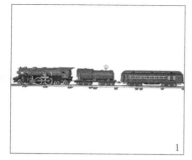

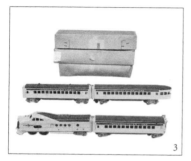

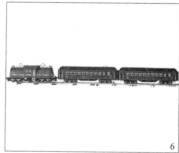

4. Marx Joy Line Set (highly appealing low-end sets), 1933–1934: Est. $250.

5. Lionel No. 9820 Sears Military Train Set, 1917–1921: $6,820—Ted Maurer's Sam Lenhart Sale, 2005.

6. Lionel Standard Gauge Large Series Passenger Set, with 381E Bild-A-Loco, 1928–1936: $18,700—Bertoia's Poch Sale I, 1999.

7. American Flyer President's Special, Wide-gauge No. 4689 locomotive in Rolls-Royce blue. 1930–1934: $8,250—Bertoia's Poch Sale I, 1999.

8. American Flyer Standard Gauge *Mayflower Set*, No. 4689 locomotive: $18,700—Bertoia's Poch Sale I, 1999.

9. Voltcamp B&O electric steeple No. 130 locomotive, early 1900s: $17,600—Barrett's Kimball Sale, 2004.

10. Märklin Boer War Armoured Train Set, 1904: Estimate $30,000.

11. Ives Wide Gauge No. 3245R *St. Paul* electric, 1930s: $20,900—Bertoia's Poch Sale II, 2000.

12. Ives *National Limited* Passenger Set, 1930: $22,000—Bertoia's Poch Sale II, 2000.

13. Ives *Princess* O-Gauge Passenger Set, No. 11 short boiler steam locomotive, 1907–1910: $10,450—Bertoia's Kuehnle Sale, 2005.

14. Lionel 2549W Northern Pacific Attack Set, w/ exploding box car, radar car; ICBM launcher, late 1950s: $1,650—Ralston's McDonough/McBride Sale, 1999.

15. Ives *White* Wide-Gauge Passenger Set, w/ No. 1132 locomotive, early 1930s: $30,800—Bertoia's Poch I Sale, 1999.

16. Ives Prosperity Special, w/ 1134 burnished copper locomotive, 1929: $55,000—Bertoia's Poch I Sale, 1999.

17. Dorfan Wide-Gauge No. 3919 Loco-Bilder locomotive; two Pullmans, 1928: Est. $3,500.

18. Märklin Ce6/8 Swiss *Crocodile* locomotive I-gauge, 1933: Est. $15,000.

9

10

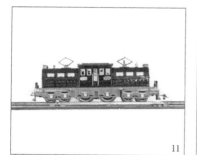

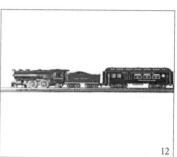

11

12

13

14

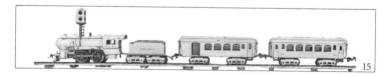

15

16

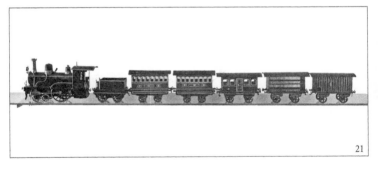

19. Märklin gauge-II clockwork *American Eagle* passenger set, with Presidential coaches, 1910: $71,500—Bertoia's Kimball Sale I, 2004. Background: Kibri Station by Kindler & Briel, early 1900.

20. Carette gauge-I 2350 locomotive & tender; rated one of the truly suberb clockwork engines made, 1910: $17,600—Barrett's Kimball Sale I, 2004.

21. Bing Gauge-4 Passenger Set, Storkleg locomotive, 1905: $42,900—Bertoia's Poch I Sale, 1999.

Hopefully the auction prices cited on these pages don't prove too intimidating. They're only a reflection of the wealth of material out there. Console yourself that many outstanding train sets are available, imbued with strong visceral impact as to patina, form, and function—yet they can still be obtained without having to "mortgage the farm."

Many of these classic entries have excelled at auction over the past five years and prices realized are included, whenever available. Bertoia's Poch Sales I and II; Kuehnle Sale; Barrett's Ward Kimball Sale I and II; and Stout and RN's Kughn Carail Collection sales will set the standard for top shelf train auctions for decades to come.

Experts' Picks

We polled some of the recognized authorities in the hobby as to what three American or European classics would rank at the top of their list.

Ken Post, Dealer/Collector, Closter, New Jersey

Ken Post is a well-known collector/dealer who served as Noel Barrett's consultant on the epic Ward Kimball Sales I and II.

"I've been collecting since I was 12 and I would rate my top three as follows: Ives' first Series 40s set, 1906. A very popular cast-iron locomotive patterned after the first large American electric, the 2-4-1 New York SI class.

Ives No. 1694 Passenger Set, 1932—a scarce transitional set, and one of the last produced by Ives before they closed their doors; only 200 produced. (See additional data in Three R's chapter.)

Lionel 1950 Golden Anniversary Set, two Union Pacific Alco Diesel No. 027 series locos in stunning orange and black; still reasonably priced but simply a great-looking set.

Ted Maurer, Train Auctioneer, Phoenixville, Pennsylvania

Ted is the acknowledged dean of toy train auctioneers, having started part-time while he was still teaching in 1966, some forty years ago. He conducts some

90 to 100 train sales a year, including a recent 35th annual post-Thanksgiving event that featured the renowned Sam Lenhart Collection (see Market Overview chapter).

"I'm sticking with prewar Standard and Wide gauge: I'd start with the Lionel No. 408 State Set in two-tone brown, 1929. One of the most elaborate sets ever produced by Lionel. Then with Ives, it'd be a tossup between the National Limited with 4-4-2 red electric steam loco and red tender or the No. 1134 Prosperity Special 4-4-2, copper-plated set from the 1929. With American Flyer, I'd choose either the Flying Colonial or the President's Special from 1928."

Glenn Ralston, of Lloyd Ralston Auctions, Stratford, Connecticut

Glenn Ralston and brother Jeff have taken the reins of the toy and train auction house started by their father, the late Lloyd Ralston, in the 1980s. As "chips off the old block," both sons are also inveterate train collectors. Glenn Ralston listed the following as his favorites:

The Lionel *Blue Comet* 1006, 1930 (named after a real comet), followed by the American Flyer *Presidential Special*, 1928, and the Ives No. 3243 *Banker's Special* in bright orange.

Stuart Waldman, Dealer/Collector, Staten Island, New York

Waldman has been at the forefront of many auction bidding duels through the years. He serves as train consultant for Bertoia Auctions, most recently at the Bernard Kuehnle Estate Sale in November 2005.

"My favorites also have a lot to do with the historical significance attached to them.

First there's the Ives *Prosperity Special* No. 1134, intended to mark the end of a golden era, but ironically introduced several weeks prior to the stock market crash in 1929. The ill-fated Special failed to sell in a depressed market and Ives' fortunes took an irreversable nosedive.

"The fabled Märklin *Armoured Train* Set, in O, I, and II gauge, 1904, was inspired by a so-named prototype

operated by the British in the Boer War in South Africa. The Boers attacked the train at Frere and captured Winston Churchill, then a war correspondent. Churchill's subsequent daring escape from a Pretoria prison made world headlines; he later wrote a book on his Boer War escapades.

"Märklin *American Eagle* Gauge II passenger set, clockwork, American steam outline; 0-4-0 loco, with U.S. flag decals, 1896. Made specifically for the U.S. market and modeled after a prototype that carried President William McKinley and his entourage campaigning on a whistle-stop tour across the country."

Bill Driscoll, Dealer/Collector, Bath, New Hampshire

Driscoll, who's currently Secretary of the Ammonoosuc Valley R.R. Assoc., has been active in the hobby since 1972, starting out in HO and switching to O scale two years later. He's been at it since he was seven or eight years old. His favorites hail from his own O-scale collection—a tie between a *Southern Pacific* 4-10-2 brass steam locomotive set with three cylinders by Max Gray, ca. 1962, and a *Sunset* brass steam locomotive set by Katsumi, Japan, also 1962. His next choice, a famous cab forward *Southern Pacific* AC-4-12 (minus the AC-9), is a two-engine 4-8-8-2 locomotive by Samhongsa, Korea, from 1992. To make it a Southern Pacific trifecta, Driscoll chose a 2-6-0 *Mogul* set in from 1985 by Max Gray. ∎

6

A SAMPLING OF TRAINS AND THEIR PRICES

Note that the following exceptional toy trains are presented by category; e.g., Steam, Tinplate, Cast-iron, Pressed Steel, Electric. Rolling stock, railside accessories, terminals are also delineated.

Top Tinplate Clockwork Trains

Alps (Japan) *San Francisco Streetcar*, No. 41, 8 in. high by 25 in. long, 1950s: $350.

Bing (Ger.) Gauge I *Hospital Train* with Wabash Engine, 1910: $3,575.

George Brown (U.S.) *Orion* loco, integral tender; two cars marked "Baltimore R.R.," yellow cab, green black, orange, 1870s: $7,500.

Buchner (Ger.) locomotive and open-seated carriage; green cabless loco with yellow/black carriage, 1865: $22,000.

Carette (Ger.) Storkleg Set, 1907: $2,500.

American Flyer boxed *Edmunds-Metzel* **O-gauge passenger set,** with No. 2 clockwork locomotive, three *Chicago* cars plus station & other accessories: $2,475— Bertoia's Kuehnle Sale, 2005.

Fallows (U.S.) *America* locomotive, cast-iron wheels; high stack, 1870s: $5,000.

Ives (U.S.) *Jumbo* locomotive , red, blue, gilt lettering, 18-½ in. long, 1885: $3,500.

Märklin (Ger.) gauge-1 *Limited Vestibule Express* 0-4-0 passenger set; early 1900s: $25,300.

Merriam (U.S.) *Progress,* blue, red, black, 15 in. long, 1880s: $2,500.

Schoener (Ger.) III-gauge train set, engine with two baggage cars; one of the first to run on track, 1894: $2,500.

Cast-Iron Trains

Carpenter (U.S.) No. 6 Engine and Coal Car high stack and large cow catcher; bright red with green trim,1890s: $2,500

Dent (U.S.) Steam Outline 4-4-0 Loco, black with gilt trim and molded ribbing; black tender with orange and gilt trim, New York Central & Hudson River in gilt relief; eight arch-cut windows in passenger cars, 1905: $2,500.

Harris (U.S.) Steam Outline M.C.R.R. *Gondola Train,* loco, tender black with gilt cowcatcher; bell, whistle; pair arch-cut windows; two yellow gondolas, caboose, 1903: $3,000.

Hubley (U.S) *No. 4 Elevated Railway* cast-iron loco, coaches have iron frames, tin bodies tender; double-track; key wind; four pylon 30-in. dia. elevated track; ptd. 1893; a record: $19,800.

Ives (U.S.) No. 188-A *White Train* (aka *Ghost Train*) locomotive; tender and two white Vestibule cars; 41 in. long, 1890s: $4,500.

Kenton (U.S.) *Camelback* #600 loco, 2-6-0 (replica of a New Jersey Central double-boiler loco) six wheels, ca. 1912: $2,000.

Pratt & Letchworth (U.S.) No. 999 *Buffalo Express* or *Vestibule Train* No. 880 loco with tender, two coaches; 60 in. long, 1892: $4,500.

Jerome Secor (U.S) clockwork locomotive, crank wound, first cast-iron engine, patented June 8, 1880: $5,000.

Wallworks (G.B.) Pull-along No. 1893 locomotive 4-2-2, with six-wheel Express tender, 1890s; one of the few cast-iron trains made by a firm outside U.S.: $1,500

Wilkins (U.S.) *Largest Train* Set, early 1900s; loco, tender, two coaches, 55 in. long, ca. 1890: $2,500.

Pressed-Steel Trains and Pedal Cars
Pressed-Steel Trains

American National (U.S.) *No. 9 Locomotive* Pedal Car, 1920s: $4,500

Buddy "L" (U.S.) *Burlington Zephyr* locomotive, red, white, 30 in. 1935: $8,250.

Buddy "L" (U.S.) *Industrial* Train Set , black, 10-in. locomotive; five cars at 6 inches; track included, 1930s: $2,200.

Cor-Cor (U.S.) Riding Locomotive, integral tender and two Pullman coaches; 1930s, 72 in. long; red and black: $2,000.

Dayton (U.S.) *Hill-Climber* Locomotive, with tender; friction power; red, black, 1920: $900.

Garton (U.S.) *Casey Jones* No. 9, locomotive and tender; steel with pneumatic tires; black and white, 32 in. long, 1961: $900.

Gendron, or possibly Pioneer (U.S.) *No. 68* engine pedal locomotive, with rubber-tired spoked wheels; functioning bell, whistle, lantern, 57 in. long, 1890s: $1,100

Keystone (U.S.) *No. 6400* Ride-em Locomotive, 2-4-2, with tender, side brake, saddle seat on cab; wooden handlebar; red, black, yellow lettering, 1920: $3,000

Lines (G.B.) Pedal Locomotive 1920; high cab: spoke wheels, bell; black, 1920: $12,000.

Marx (U.S.) *Cannonball Express* No. 9, 1940s: $750.

Steelcraft (U.S.) *20th Century Limited* No. 285 Riding Locomotive Deluxe; 1937; *Express Car De Luxe* No. 286, 23¾ in. long; 1937: $5,000 the set.

Toledo Wheel Goods (U.S.) *Fast Mail* loco red, black trim, white lettering; 42½ in. long, 1930s $2,500.

Velo-King (U.S.) Pedal Locomotive No. 67, ca. 1880: $2,000.

Steam Trains

Beggs (U.S) live steam *Passenger set* with *U.S. Mail* Postal Car, 12 in. overall, 1890: $5,225.

Bing (Ger.) *Charles Dickens* passenger set w/European outline live steam locomotive, tender, and three parlor cars; original six-wick burner, 1890s. $41,800.

Hubley No. 4 Elevated Railway cast-iron locomotive and coaches (left); track, 30 in. dia.; patented 1893; a record $19,800; **George Brown Excelsior tin clockwork locomotive** (right), 1870s: $3,300—Barrett's Kimball Sale II, 2005.

Bing (Ger.) *Gauge-IV Passenger Set*; steam-powered Stork-leg loco; green, red/black and silver trim; original box, largest of Bing's steam series, 1900: $42,900.

Carette (Ger.) *Gauge-III Passenger Set*; 4-2-0-steam outline green w/gun metal boiler and red trim; matching tender; baggage car, sleeping car, brown and green: $16,500 at Bertoia's Poch I, 1999.

Märklin (Ger.) #2609 gauge-III live steam 4-4-0 locomotive and tender; with original wood box: $82,500 (a record for engine and tender).

Newton (G.B.) locomotive 2-2-2 and tender, 1890s: $6,500.

Ernst Plank (Ger.) *Vulcan* engine, painted tin, gauge III with brass boiler; live steam, passenger set includes tender, two cars: $46,750

Jean Schoenner (Ger.) Passenger Train set, in almost unheard of 90 mm, the largest gauge for this model; American outline; 4-2-2 locomotive; 4-wheeled tender, 1890s: $19,800.

Weeden (U.S.) *Dart* Train Set, black, red, yellow steam loco, black, red tender, red coach with box; track section, and pair of water pouring pans; 23 in. long: $3,500.

Lithograph Paper-on-Wood Trains

Rufus Bliss (U.S.) *Adirondack R.R.* train set, locomotive has number "61"; baggage express car and *Saratoga* coach, 28 in. long; each car is filled with flat alphabet blocks, 1889–1895: $3,500.

Rufus Bliss (U.S.) *World Columbian Palace* Car, unnamed locomotive, "W.C.S.T."-marked tender; 12-wheel coach; 40 in. long overall, 1893: $3,500.

Rufus Bliss (U.S.) *Empire State Express*, 4-4-4 locomotive with 12-wheel passenger coach, 1895: $2,500.

Milton Bradley (U.S.) *Hercules* locomotive, tender, and Atlantic & Pacific R.R parlor car, 1890s: $3,500.

Milton Bradley (U.S.) *Reindeer* Train; made to be assembled in puzzle fashion; locomotive, tender, four circus cage cars; cars bear names of various wild animals, 45 in. overall, 1890s: $5,000.

Erzgeberge (Ger.) Freight Train set; loco, two flatcars and caboose, 1870: $850.

Fisher-Price (U.S.) *Mickey Mouse Choo-Choo* locomotive, 1938: $1,000.

W.S. Reed (U.S.) *Mother Goose* Rail Road, ca. 1895; locomotive, tender, and passenger car with lithographed Mother Goose figures peering out from passenger car; 38 in. long, ca. 1895: $3,500.

W.S. Reed (U.S.) *Duke* loco; Reed's Drawing Room Car, plus tender, 1890, 45 in. overall: $3,000.

C.H. Sheperd (U.S.) *Curve Railroad Coal Route* Pennsylvania Set, boxed set includes two locomotives, two coal cars, and track, boxed, ca. 1885: $2,200.

Novelty Trains
Clockwork and Electric

Chein (U.S.) *Krazy Kat Express* Train pull toy, screen printed and painted wood, Krazy Kat's head projects from top of engine cab, 12 in., 1932: $2,500.

Hercules Metal Line (U.S.) *Popeye & Olive Oyl* Handcar; made for Marx, tin with rubber figures; made a tin gauge-O version and a flangeless tin toy floor train, 1935. No price available.

Lionel (U.S.) No. 1103 *Peter Rabbit & Chick Mobile*; O gauge; Peter Rabbit is at controls of handcar; Easter basket mounted on other end; 1935–1937: $2,500 (Bertoia, Nov., #1286).

Lionel (U.S.) *Santa Claus* handcar; Santa, with Mickey Mouse in his sack, pumps while Yule tree is on opposite end of car, 1935–1936: $5,000.

Marx (U.S.) Girard handcar (uncataloged); lithographed tin windup; two railroad workers, 1933–1935: $350

Marx (U.S.) *Moon Mullins and Kayo* Handcar, die-cut jointed flat tin figures of comic-strip duo, Kayo stands on top of dynamite box; 6 in. long; 1930s: $1,500.

Marx (U.S.) *Flintstones Bedrock Express*, zig-zag train: $200.

Marx (U.S.) *Popeye Express*, 1940s, Popeye in airplane circles colorful lithographed 9 in. dia. track layout, where a tiny express train negotiates tunnels and speeds along track. Includes colorful box and inserts, 1940s: $3,500.

Marx (U.S.) Walt Disney's *Mickey Mouse Meteor* Train Set, mid-1930s, loco features Donald Duck and three nephews, clockwork, 43 in. long, 1935: $3,000.

Second version illustrates Mickey and Minnie Mouse, Goofy and Doc from movie *Snow White:* $4,000.

Nifty (Ger.) *Toonerville Trolley* tin clockwork car; 6¾ in. high; 1922: $2,000

Wells-Brimtoy (G.B) *Cinderella Rail Car;* composition mice from movie *Cinderella* operate clockwork handcar; box, track, shows Wells of London (G.B.), Mickey and Minnie Mouse Handcar, clockwork, boxed 1930s hand-painted composition figures of Mickey and Minnie, 7¼ in. high; box 14 in.: $3,500

Electric Trolleys

Carette (Ger.) Street Car running on dry-cell or wet-cell batteries. Later Carette offered a 4-wheeled tram and an exotic 8-wheeled tram, 1892: $3,000.

Carlisle & Finch (U.S.) Tram, shiny copper and nickel, 1899: $1,200.

Ives (U.S.) *Local Suburban Service* No. 800, O-gauge Trolley, 1909: $11,600.

Kenco (U.S.) *Pleasure Ave.* Trolley, painted maroon/gray roof, raised white lettering; electric motor, 8 in. long, 1920s: $5,225

Lionel (U.S.) Electric Trolley Standard Gauge No. 4, ca. 1908, double motors; yellow: $8,500

Lionel (U.S.) #29 *Day Coach Trolley*, N.Y.C. & H.R R.R. Co., 1912: $9,487.

Lionel (U.S.) *City Hall Park Trolley*; 1902; second electric-powered toy in Lionel line; 17 in. long; light steel superstructure was contracted out to Morton Converse, known for similar trolleys, 1902: $31,900.

Märklin (Ger.) *New York* steam car, I gauge, uncataloged (extremely scarce; one of only a few known in this gauge to be fitted with a motor), 1912: $8,000.

Märklin (Ger.) *Summer Coach*, enameled with highed roof and composition passengers, ca. 1910, $26,400.

Märklin (Ger.) Trolley Electrische Strassenbahn #8, gauge I, non-motorized, 1909: $12,500.

Märklin (Ger.) *Union Traction Co.,* Trolley made for U.S. market; large key wind on roof; 12½ in. long, ca. 1890s, ex-Krames collection: $49,500

Voltamp (U.S.) #2115 *Interurban Trolley;* 13 in. long; painted tin with wood-framed and cast-iron trucks, wheels, and pilots, wooden seats: $35,200

Electric Locomotives and Train Sets

The following represent another array of true classics that many collectors might well feel belong in the earlier Blue Ribbon section.

Aster (U.S) *Big Boy Union Pacific* Live Steam Locomotive, 1/32 scale, 1941–1942: $10,500.

American Flyer (U.S.) *The Statesman* set, orange w/orange cars, 4654, 4151-4151-4152; 1928. No price available.

American Flyer (U.S.) *All American* No.1433 Set; wide gauge maroon 4019, 4040, 4041, 4042 cars, 1925. No price available.

American Flyer (U.S.) *Burlington Zephyr Streamliner*, #9900, O gauge, lithographed tin engine w/ two coaches, silver finish with black side-striping, mid-1930s: $1200.

Boucher (U.S.) #2100 *Locomotive Freight* Set, 1930s: $12,650.

Fulgerex Scale Model brass #241 Locomotives, O and HO gauge; handmade by firm owned by noted collector Count Giansanti Coluzzi: $22,000 .

Howard (U.S.) Pennsylvania RR 2-rail electric; locomotive with U.S. Mail Car, two passenger cars, ca 1910: $37,400

Ives (U.S.) *Halloween Set* No. 3236 loco; 184 club car, 186 observation car; with set boxes, ca 1929: $3,080,

Ives (U.S.) O-gauge *Major H.O.D. Seagrave* Special Deluxe Set: #1122, 4-4-2 loco, matching tender, two parlor cars and observation car—all done in gleaming copper plating, nickeled roofs: $4,950 at Bertoia's Poch I Sale, Oct. 1999.

Ives (U.S.) O-gauge Red *Circus* Train set, #1122 loco, 4-4-2 with matching tender; yellow flatcar piggy-backing pair of circus wagon cars, 1931 (one of Ive's last hurrahs and the only known example): $27,500 at Bertoia's Poch I Sale, Oct. 1999.

Ives (U.S.) 3243R *Wanamaker Railroad Lines* department store special loco and cars; mid-1920s: $19,250

Ives (U.S.) *Twentieth Century Limited* Set; loco, tender, three cars: $28,600 at Barrett's Kimball Sale II, May 2005.

Lehmann Gross Bahn (Ger.) *100th. Anniversary Set,* 1981, brawny G-scale entry has appreciated as much as 20 times in value since its debut. No price available.

Leland (U.S.) *Mono Elevated* 2000, pressed steel, three cars and rail system; cars 8¼ in. long: $2,420 at Bertoia's Poch Sale I.

Lionel (U.S.) Standard-gauge *Large Series* Passenger Set No. 381E *Bild-A-Loco*, 1928–1936; 12-wheel loco, so underpowered, it was abruptly withdrawn and replaced by a twin engine No. 402. The 381E is still hotly pursued despite a recent excellent Williams replication: $16,500 *at Bertoia's Poch I Sale, 1999.*

Lionel (U.S.) Baltimore & Ohio No. 5, Lionel's first electric loco; also the first to be modeled after a prototype, 1901: $5,500.

Lionel (U.S.) *Boy's Set* 1955, limited production (today only four are known); an example sold at Greenberg's Vendetti collection sale for $23,000, Nov. 1988.

Lionel (U.S.) O-gauge *Streamline Passenger* set with twin #2373 *Canadian Pacific* Diesel, including *Banff Park* and two *Silver Dawn* observation cars, 1957: $4,950 at NETTE, June 2005.

Postwar Lionels—1945–1980

A number of the following classics appeared on a list of top 20 postwar Lionels compiled by writer/collector Joe Algozzini as his personal favorites in *Classic Toy Trains Magazine* in the Summer 1989 issue. The article triggered intense reader reaction from Lionel loyalists. One irate collector insisted that Lionel's greatest (postwar) years were 1946, 1950, and 1955. He felt that almost every good item since is a variation of trains issued in those three years and one could forget anything made after 1958. What it finally comes down to is that the true favorites, the dream trains among collectors, are often the first set each of us received as a child, or that one set we didn't get as a child.

Lionel (U.S.) *No. 224 Steamer* with tender, four coaches; first and only set offered in firm's catalog in 1945, the year the war ended.

Lionel (U.S.) *No. 726 Berkshire* 2-8-4 with numerous nice trimmings, 1946; three Irvington passenger cars.

Lionel (U.S.) *Pennsylvania GG1*, 4-6-6-4 electric loco patterned after the classic Ray Lowey–designed prototype; often hailed as Lionel's most glamorous postwar entry.

Lionel (U.S.) *No. 2025 Pacific* 2-6-2 steam outline with whistling tender, black, 1947.

Lionel Santa Fe Twin diesel, O-gauge, 1948, bright silver and red markings; scale model of the General Motors prototype. Set retailed at a whopping $199.50.

Lionel (U.S.) two *Union Pacific Alco Diesel No. 027* passenger and freight series: The Anniversary Set, 1950; bright orange and black locos. Also marking Lionel's 50th anniversary, the No. 773 *Hudson* classic.

Lionel (U.S.) Pennsylvania R.R. Congressional with No. 2340 Tuscan red GG1 tender, and *Molly Pitcher, William Penn, Betsy Ross,* and *Alexander Hamilton* passenger cars, 1955.

Lionel (U.S.) *Jersey Central Train Master*, 1956, with wide channel passenger cars; one of the most sought-after postwar locos, it is often reproduced.

Lionel (U.S.) *Burlington No. 2328,* four-car set with distinctive red stripes. Modeled after General Motors or Fairbanks Morse prototypes,1956.

Collectors cite 1957 as a landmark year, headed by one of the most striking Lionels to hit the rails—the *Canadian Pacific Super O Luxury Liner* set, including the *Hudson* and five cars, with two added Pullmans, *Blair Manor* and *Craig,* available separately;

Lionel (U.S.) *Mount Rushmore* corner train layout set: $13,800 at RM Auction Kughn Carail Sale, 2003.

Lionel (U.S.) *U.S. Marines No. 1625* military 0-4-0 set with three flatcars with toy military vehicles made by Pyro; Gray No. 6017-85 caboose is a tough one to track down; 1958.

Lionel (U.S.) *Virginian* and *Owl* rectifier freight set with the ever-elusive *No. 6556 Katy* stock car and No. 6427-60 *Virginian* caboose. 1958.

Lionel (U.S.) *#2511W* train set; a 3252 EP-5 loco pulling five freight cars, 1958: $7,810 at NETTE, June 2005.

Lionel (U.S.) No. 1882 uncataloged *Halloween* Set; private label sets for various retail stores such as Sears, Macy's, and Ward's are highly sought after. This 1960 entry by an unknown marketer is another "keeper."

Lionel (Sears) (U.S.) *No. 9820 Military Train* Set, with scarce flatcar with tank, No. 3666 cannon box car, and No. 347 cannon firing range set and toy soldiers, 1964.

Two more recent Lionel entries that belong in any advanced post-war collection include the Lionel *SD60M Conrail* Set, from 1994 and the Lionel SD80MAC, from 2002.

Märklin (Ger.) *Kaiser* I-Gauge Passenger set. 1914: $11,000 at Bertoia's Poch Sale I, 1999.

Märklin gauge-I *Royal Blue Limited* passenger train; 16-in.-long engine and tender; cars are 9½ in. long; $50,600 at Barrett's Ward Kimball Sale, May 2005.

Two limited editions (5,000 issued) by Märklin (Ger.): the *Ontario National R.R. Northlander No. 3150* diesel loco four car train, 0-4-4-0, 1978, bright blue plastic bodies, black roofs; demand was so great that repro models have surfaced (originals are numbered and have factory certificates). Also the *Belgium BR96 No. 3101 Tank* locomotive, 2-6-0 in green, black plastic.

Märklin (Ger.) *Central London Railway,* 1906, gauges O, I, and II; 8-wheel engine; modeled after London underground railway system prototypes

Märklin (Ger.) *Armoured* train set, 1904, crude, squared-off locomotive; open car for soldiers and a cannon car patterned after Boer War prototypes; gauges I, O, and II, and possibly III (cannon car could be pushed ahead of loco and used to clear the tracks by firing cap guns activated by the rails).

Märklin (Ger.) *gauge-I passenger set*, 4-4-0, clockwork locomotive with two presidential coaches in deep blue with painted stars and stripes; hinged roofs and bench seating; considered the first Märklin clockwork loco made for U.S. market: $71,500 at Barrett's Kimball Sale I, Nov. 2004.

Märklin Swiss Fed. R.R. *Ce6/8 electric loco, Crocodile* I-gauge; first appeared in 1933; a widely popular miniaturized OO-Gauge version was introduced by Märklin in 1947.

Marx (U.S.) *Army Supply Train*, 1940 with No. 500 tender, olive, gold.

Ernst Plank (Ger) brass, green, red painted tin locomotive with high cab, 1882. Possibly the first true electric toy train: $15,000 est.

Voltamp (U.S.) Pennsylvania passenger set, loco 14 in. long; scarce deep maroon variant; both cars have wooden seats; cars 13 in. long: $24,200 at Barrett's Kimball Sale I, Nov. 2005.

Rolling Stock

Bing (Ger.) I-gauge Liquid Car, with box: $2,200 at Barrett's Harling Sale, May 2003.

Carette (Ger.) *Coleman's Mustard* I-gauge truck in distinctive bright yellow and royal coat of arms; for British market, 1910.

Carlisle & Finch (U.S.) 52-passenger coach: $3,740 at Stout Auction, Dec. 2004.

Dorfan (U.S.) #3931 brown caboose, 1930s: $4,565 at Stout Auction, Dec. 2004.

Fundimensions (U.S.) *Toy Fair* boxcar No.7817, red, white, blue with cameo oval portrait of Joshua Lionel Cowen, 1980.

Knapp (U.S.) Fast Freight #236 Caboose: $2,650 at Bertoia's Poch Sale I, 1999.

Lionel (U.S.) #6464-100 *Western Pacific* boxcar in orange and blue, 1954 (only six known): a record $74,250 at Stout Auction's Toy & Train Sale in Dec. 2004.

Lionel (U.S.) #6464-300 *Rutland* Box Car, with box: $21,150 at Stout Auction's Toy & Train Sale, Dec. 2004.

Lionel (U.S.) *Dummy Crane Car*, in 2⅞ in. gauge; early 1900s; cast-iron frame with tin platform, hand crank and ratchet brake; made in 9 or 10 different models, some with subtle variations: $46,200 at Barrett's Kimball Sale I, Nov. 2004.

Lionel (U.S.) *Irvington No. 2625* O-gauge passenger car, 1946–1949; green variant is highly uncommon and goes for $5,000 (est.) more than 10 times that of the tuscan color ($250–300.)

Lionel (U.S.) No. 800 *Jail Car*, an early 2⅞-in. gauge box-car, so-called because it has bars on its windows, ca.1905: $8,800 at Ralston's McDonough/McBride Sale, 1999.

Märklin (Ger.) *Armoured Gun Car* (from classic 1904 Boer War set), 8 in. long: $21,100 at Barrett's Kimball Sale II, May 2005.

Märklin (Ger.) I-gauge crane car with brass broiler : $30,800 at Barrett's John Harling Sale, July 2003.

Märklin (Ger.) I-gauge hand-enameled *Hospital* Car: $4,030 at NETTE, Jan. 2004.

Train Stations

Ives (U.S.) *Grand Central Station,* lithograph tin; covered platform with stained glass ceiling panels; 18½ in. long, 1930s: $6,050.

Ives (U.S.) *Union Station*, tin lithographed; depicts ticket office; waiting passengers, 1930s: $1,430.

Ives (U.S.) (untitled) Train Station with 32 panel covered platform: $24,200.

Märklin (Ger.) *Durchgang Station*; painted tin; 17½ inches long; extensive detail with central dome on roof; red/pale green, gold : $2,860 at Bertoia's Poch I Sale, 1999.

Märklin (Ger.) *Leipsig Station*; multi-windowed cupola, yellow and brown; central steps and approach walkways; 19½ in. high × 20½ in. long: $23,100

Märklin (Ger.) *Casino* with Victorian details: $4,620,

Märklin (Ger.) *Café Station* (so named for its adjoining terrace, outfitted with dining tables and chairs); early 1900s; unusual three-sided roof shelters terrace and visitors; also a three-sided ticket booth 14 in. high including clock tower, 12 in. wide by 14 in. deep: $20,900

Märklin (Ger.) *Bradford Station*, in enameled embossed tin; corrugated tin platform canopy; Refreshment Room has bench, chairs, candleholder; glazed and stained-glass windows. Missing ramps: $20,900

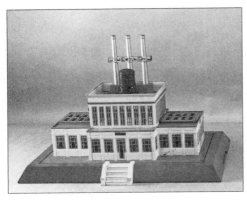

Montage of Märklin bridges, 1920s & 1930s Barrett's Kimball Sale II, 2005.
Lionel Power Station No. 840, boxed, 1950s: $2,310—Bertoia Poch Sale I, 1999.
Lionel water tower ($112) & No. 455 oil derrick ($84), 1950s—Morphy Toy Sale, 2005.

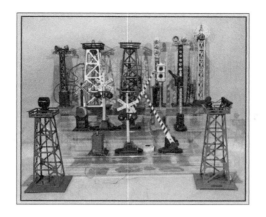

Märklin (Ger.) (untitled) Station with glass platform canopy, 1895; hand finished trompe l'oeil painting with faux wood doors; 14 in. high,19 in. wide × 10 in. deep: $49,500 at Barrett's Kimball Sale I, 2004

Märklin *Gere de Versailles*, gauge I, embossed tin station, featured in *Trains of Avenue de Rumine* by Count Giasanti Coluzzi: $20,900 at Noel Barrett Toy Auction, Oct, 1997.

Märklin "Necessary," enameled tinplate with Elastolin lady figure: $412.50 at Noel Barrett Toy Auction, Oct. 1997.

Marx (U.S.) *No. 2940 Grand Central Station*, ca. 1939; swinging doors, illuminated, 10¾ in. high by 17 in. long: $500.

Marx (U.S.) *No. 1600 Glendale Depot* with battery-operated crossing gates, 1940s: $250.

Railside Accessories

Bing (Ger.) Overhead Crane, revolving with workman's cab; girder tower houses electric motor which controls chain and electromagnet: $3,300

Bing (Ger.) clockwork bridge for gauge-O trains; perhaps a factory protype since it does not appear in catalogs: $14,300.

Märklin (Ger.) Tin Streetlight with ladder, spirit fired lamp with glass globe: $12,100

Märklin (Ger.) Girder Bridge (replaced lamps and missing flags): $29,700.

Rock & Graner Nachfolger (Ger.) footbridge with four signals; each base has small pierced tin bench; a companion piece to the station listed above; 1900s: $44,000.

Ives (U.S.) Powerhouse #200, lithographed tin faux brick with removable chimney; 11 in. long × 12½ in. high., 1930s: $850.

Märklin Elevated Goods Platform, Gauge I, enameled and embossed 1920s: $25,300— Barrett's Kimball Sale I.

Dorfan Elevated Crane, 20 in. high: $11,000— Bertoia's Poch Sale I, 1999.

Lionel (U.S.) 2⅞ gauge cast-iron trestle bridge, steel strip track, and wood ties, 24 in. long, ca. 1903: $3,500.

Lionel (U.S.) *Operating Bascule Bridge #313*; cream and red gateman's house, 1940s: $440.

Lionel (U.S.) *No. 300 Hellgate Bridge*, orange, cream, green: $1,100.

Lionel (U.S.) *Scenic Park*; decorative landscaped three-section plot board with various tinplate homes, bungalows, and country estates; 85 in. long: $10,120.

(German, maker unknown) *Engine House* with three track bays; large-scale roundhouse; in green painted tinplate; 21 × 12½ in.: $715.

Lionel (U.S.) *Weighing Scale #441*; 29½ in. long: $2,090.

Lionel (U.S.) Railroad Crossing Stop sign: $3,680

Märklin (Ger.) Street Lamp, Victorian style, 18 in. high; polychrome cast-iron base, early 1900s: $3,300. ◾

7

THE INSTANT EXPERT QUIZ

1. What is the width between the inner rails of a toy train track called?

2. The most popular toy railroading category is: (check one)

   a. by material and motive power (e.g., tinplate, cast iron, die-cast, pressed steel; steam, clockwork, electric)

   b. by period; e.g., Classic 1923–1940, Post–World War II, Contemporary

   c. by gauge and scale; e.g., Standard, Wide, Narrow, HO, Z

   d. by manufacturer and country of origin; e.g., Lionel, U.S.; Märklin, Ger.

3. One of Märklin's all time classics, the 1933 Swiss Federated R.R.'s Ce6/8, was named after what fearsome reptile?

4. Two train museums have been dedicated to the legendary engineer Casey Jones. Where are they located?

5. The best way for absentee bidders to win a desired train lot at auction is—what?

6. An American outline locomotive with a smoke stack or chimney, double-coned to cool off sparks is called—what?

7. What category of trains (parlor toys, clockwork, steam, electric) is least prone to the market's cyclical glitches and appears to be recession proof?

8. What toy maker produced clockwork train sets in the early 1900s that were almost an exact copy image of Issmayer's?

9. What fallen flag (defunct rail line) known as "a mighty good road," is celebrated in a Leadbelly folk classic?

10. What classic early-1900s piece of rolling stock was hand assembled in the owner's workshop and recently made auction history at $46,200?

11. What item classified as ephemera is the single most feverishly pursued toy train adjunct, sometimes bringing prices comparable to the train sets they depict?

12. What novelty key wind train set featuring Mickey Mouse became one of Marx's hottest sellers in the postwar period?

13. What U.S. train manufacturers were known as the "Big Four"?

14. What leading train maker introduced the Hummer clockwork cast-iron locomotive in 1916?

15. What hallowed toy firm, founded in 1881, made a belated entry into toy train making in 1968, nearly 90 years later?

16. What firm; known for a line of electrical novelties, issued one of the earliest electric trams in 1899?

17. What was the name of Lionel's most popular locomotive, bearing NYC livery and introduced in 1937?

18. Fundimension, which bought out Lionel, issued a Toy Fair Box Car No. 7817 in 1980 that bore an oval portrait of what personage?

19. What well-known publishing firm and show promoter has issued over 20 train manufacturer reference guides since the 1970s?

20. Because classics such as its *Champion Limited* are so highly esteemed, collectors excuse the use of replacement bodies on which firm's locomotives?

Answers:

1. Gauge.—See *Creating a Complete Model Railway System.*

2. (d) By manufacturer & country of origin.—See *Finding Your Collecting Groove.*

3. The *Crocodile.* See *Toy and Model Train History.*

4. Museums are located in Vaughan, Miss., and Jackson, Tenn.—See *Railroads and Museums.*

5. Submit a ceiling bid that's clearly on the high side.—See *Buying and Selling Trains at Auction.*

6. Diamond stacker.—See *Glossary.*

7. Electric trains.—See *Market Overview.*

8. Ives, Blakeslee & Co.—See *The Three R's—Repros, Repaints, Restorations.*

9. Rock Island Line (Chicago, Rock Island & Pacific R.R.).—See *Leading Flag and Common Railway Acronyms.*

10. The Lionel *Dummy crane* car, hand-assembled by Joshua Cowen.—See *Behind the Great Finds and Storied Collections.*

11. Train manufacturers catalogs.—See *Railroadiana.*

12. *Mickey Mouse Meteor Train* Set, 1950–1951.—See *Toy and Model Train History.*

13. American Flyer, Lionel, Ives, and Marx.—See *Toy and Model Train History.*

14. American Flyer.—See *Manufacturer's Listing.*

15. Lehmann (Lehmann Gross Bahn).—See *Manufacturer's Listing.*

16. Carlisle & Finch.—See *Portfolio of Blue Ribbon Trains.*

17. The *Hudson No. 700E.*—See *Portfolio of Blue Ribbon Trains.*

18. Lionel founder Joshua Lionel Cowen.—See *Portfolio of Blue Ribbon Trains.*

19. Greenberg Publishing Co.—See *Bibliography.*

20. Dorfan, whose zinc-cast locomotives suffered a high mortality rate due to metal fatigue.—See *The Three R's—Repros, Repairs, Restorations.* ◼

RESOURCE GUIDE

GLOSSARY

Action cars
Rolling stock, dating from the 1950s and 1960s intended for active play, that defied realism and bore little resemblance to real life examples. Included flatcars bearing fire-fighting derricks and ladders, helicopters, tanks, rockets, radar antennas, missiles, anti-aircraft guns, and other weaponry.

Alcos
Acronym for American Locomotive Company which made diesel and electric locomotives and switches. A number of Lionel locomotives replicated ALCO prototypes.

American
Designation for 4-4-0 wheel configuration.

Animated toys or trains
Any plaything that simulates lifelike movements, whether activated by springs, string, flywheel, rubber band, gravity, controlled movement of sand, gyroscope, steam, electricity, or batteries.

Articulated
Steam locomotive with two sets of driving wheels and cylinders which pivot on separate frames.

Atlantic
Another name for 4-4-2 wheel arrangement. Its counterpart, the Pacific, is configured 4-6-2.

Bi-polar
A type of electric locomotive innovated by Minn. & St. Paul R.R. in 1920; served as a prototype by virtually every major U.S. train model manufacturer.

Bird cage
Raised roof section for guard's lookout in certain vintage coaches or vans.

Block
A section of track designated for purpose of controlling trains.

Bogie
British term for low-truck, free swiveling assembly in front or behind a locomotive's driving wheels. American term is truck.

Bunker
Container for coal on a tank engine.

Bury
An early primitive looking locomotive with 0-4-0 wheel configuration, so named after an obscure train maker.

Cab-forward
American steam locomotive type with cab at head-end.

Caboose
Rear car that often houses guards, workmen, and equipment. British refer to as van. In railroad lingo, a caboose is a hack or shanty.

Camelback
Locomotive with cab astride the boiler; the fireman rode under the hood in the rear; also called a Mother Hubbard.

Carpet runner
Motorless tin, cast-iron, copper, or sheet-steel locomotive or train set with smooth wheel rims, not grooved to run on tracks but push-pulled on the floor. Also known as floor-runner.

Cast iron
Typical material for pre-1900s locomotives and tenders. An American phenomenon, used by noted makers from Arcade to Williams. Process entails hand-pouring high carbon gray iron into sandcast

molds. Usually cast in half. Parts are then mated and bolted or riveted to form a complete toy.

Catenary
Overhead wire system supporting contact or conductor wire that provides electric current to engines and cars; power passes from catenaries to the diamond-shaped pantograph mounted atop locomotive and down to motor. Commonly used in real trains as well as toy trains.

Clerestory
Raised section of cab roof with windows or ventilators.

Climax
Type of articulated locomotive.

Clockwork
Made of brass and steel, clockwork was adopted as a drive system for toys and trains by watchmakers beginning in the 1860s. The mechanism is wound like a clock or watch, and the interlocking gears cause the train to move as spring uncoils. Able to sustain motion up to 30 minutes. Gave way to electric by World War I.

Co-Co
Diesel or electric locomotive with two six-wheeled trucks, all wheel driven; a.k.a. C.C.

Cog railway
A railroad using toothed wheels on the loco to mesh with racks between running rails; helpful in negotiating steep grades, such as the Mt. Washington Cog RR in New Hampshire. Also known as rack railroad.

Combine
Used as a noun; a basic car that may have dual functions; e.g., a mail car and a passenger coach.

Consists (pronounced CON-sists)
A group of locomotives or the makeup of the train including engine and rolling stock, usually freight cars.

Coupe-vents

Early streamlined style typical of German and French locomotives; known for V-shaped chimneys, domes, cab, and boiler front; also called wind-splitters.

Coupler

A unit that connects individual cars. Early couplers were simple locking devices such as hook (1920s) and latch (1924); later automatic couplers (1938) were both electric and mechanical. Other types: inverted T-type semiautomatic (mid-1920s), manual box-coupler (1936), FM magnet coupler (1955), link couplers and automatic knuckle couplers (1952), non-operating (1957).

Cow

Another name for a standard road switcher for EMD (Electro Motive Div.) manufactured streamlined units. The prototype is sometimes found with a B unit called a calf, appearing in scale HO train sets.

Cowcatcher

Projecting device in front of many early American locomotives to clear snow or other obstacle on the track; a.k.a. pilot.

Crossing

Special section of track that permits two tracks to cross each other but does not entail train moving from one track to a parallel track.

Crossover

Track and switches laid back to back facilitate crossing from one parallel track to another.

Cut

Several cars hooked to an engine, or coupled together by themselves. Also, a right-of-way that has been channeled across a high area, as opposed to run over it or tunneled through it.

Deadhead

To direct a train to a specific and not deploy it immediately, but position it for work later. Applies to both R.R. employees and equipment.

Decapod
Refers to a 10-wheeled clockwork model patterned after a British experimental model with that number of driving wheels.

Derail
As a verb, to go off the rails; as a noun: a device placed on track to keep cars from rolling into the main line and causing a collision.

Diamond stacker
American-type locomotive with a smoke stack or chimney, double-coned to cool off sparks.

Die-cast
Method of mass-producion; molten zinc and white metal alloys are injected into permanent molds under great pressure; later trimmed and painted. Sharp, precise detail can be achieved. Die-cast toys were very inexpensive and were generally found in department stores and hobby shops.

Dome
Round projection atop locomotive boilers which contains steam controls or sand.

Dome car
U.S. passenger car with observation dome on roof or a second deck with windows, a.k.a. Vista Dome car.

Doubleheading
Using two locomotives with two separate crews to pull a train.

Drive wheels
Wheels, also called power wheels, configured in the midle row on the truck, attached to piston rod that transmits energy from power source, as on toy locomotives.

Dummy
A unit without power fabricated by toy train firms that creates the illusion that the entire complex has pulling power. It may be a dummy tank or other component added to achieve symmetry.

Fallen flags
Classic, now defunct, railroad lines of the glorious past; e.g., New York, Ontario and Western, the Lehigh Valley; Atkchison Topeka & Sante Fe.

First generation diesels
Locomotives that replaced steam types; "second generation" applies to units built from 1960 to 1985.

Fish-plate
A bar connecting ends of rails.

Flange
Portion of railway wheel that has a protruding rim to keep the wheel on track.

Frog
Model track; a junction, grooved for wheel flanges, between two arms of a turnout or switch, originally called points; so called because it resembles a frog.

Gandy-dancer
Colorful jargon in railroad lore; refers to laborers who lay track, grade roadbeds, and such.

Gauge
Width between the inside edges of each rail, normally determined by the scale of a specific manufacturer.

Geep (pronounced "jeep")
Nickname for road switchers on General Motors GP series diesel locos, especially early models of the 1950s. Similar in profile, but slightly longer than Geeps are the SD units.

Gondola
America term for open freight car.

Goods car
Another name for freight car, usually the last car on the consist.

Head-end cars
Mail, baggage, and express cars, so named because they are usually positioned just behind the locomotive.

HEP
Acronym for Head-End Power. Refers to the front of the locomotive.

Heralds
Insignias of the legendary railways.

Highball
To speed; also a sign to proceed; so called because of old bell-shaped symbols.

Journal
The part of the shaft or axle of a train engine or car that rests on its bearings.

Journal boxes
Axles terminate in this unit, which contains bearings and lubricants to permit axle to roll freely.

Layout
A complete model railroad system comprising transformer, loco, rolling stock, terminals, power houses, railside equipment, scenery—limited solely by the imagination of the collector or modeler.

Lineside equipment
Telephone poles, crossing signals, tunnels, bridges, switches, signal towers, floodlight stanchions, water towers, unloading ramps—any material or equipment along the train's right-of-way.

Lithographed paper-on-wood
Solid wood, two-dimensional toys, including boats and trains, embellished with colorful lithographed paper glued to cut-out wood.

Locomotive
The lead car in the train set (often used interchangeably with *engine*) and the only unit containing a working power mechanism that enables it to pull the tender and other rolling stock; obviously the most vital component of any real-life or model toy train system.

Mixed train
A train carrying both passenger and freight cars.

M.O.W.
Acronym for Maintenance of Way, a specialized group of RR cars that are employed to keep the track clear of freight and passenger trains; M.O.W. work-horses include cranes, crane tenders, flatcars (carrying rails, ties), and work cabooses.

Nuremberg style
Toy trains of a distinctive rolled tinplate and tab style by makers from Nuremberg including Bing, Carette, Rock & Graner, Kraus, Issmayer, Lutz, and Bub from the late 1890s to World War I. Renowned for detail and hand-soldered, hand-painted finish.

Pantograph
Geometric-shaped steel device on real-life and model trains located atop a car or locomotive that collects electric current from overhead lines.

Piggyback
Transport of highway truck trailers or containers on R.R. flatcars.

Pressed steel
Material that is rolled into a tin plate and then stamped out and spot welded, or fitted tab in slot. Used in toys and trains as early as 1895.

Prototype
Term has double meaning. Normally it refers to a real-life train or its rolling stock on which a toy train is replicated or modeled. Toy makers tend to confuse matters by using "prototype" to denote a pre-production or display model that may or may not be added to the product line.

Pullman
A sleeping car, made by the so-named Chicago coach company; has evolved as a generic for any coach in a passenger consist.

Rake
A group of coaches, coupled to a locomotive; which make up a train or consist.

Reefer
Refrigerator cars that carry food and other perishables.

Rolling stock
All-inclusive term for cars that are pulled by the locomotive.

Roundhouse
A locomotive shed with multiple stalls, usually aligned with parking tracks that radiate from a turntable.

Scratchbuilt
Models that are hand-fashioned from start to finish.

Shunting
Moving rack or rolling stock to form train. American term is switching.

Smokestack
U.S. term for the chimney or funnel of a locomotive.

Spectacle plate
A vertical steel or brass plate found on early cabless locomotives, with two round windows resembling spectacles; unit provides protection from weather.

Splasher
A wheel cover that acts as a mudguard, preventing splashes against the locomotive and protects passengers waiting in stations.

Spring-driven
Stamped tinplate gears activated by a spring that uncoils; popularly called toy windups or keywinds. Less complex than early clockwork mechanism, they usually wind down after three or four minutes. Often rewound with a key, although a lever is known to activate certain spring-driven toy banks and toy locomotives. Windups date back to the 1890s and are still used today on low-end toys and trains.

Steam-powered toy trains
Originally considered scientific toys. Rather expensive solid-brass locomotives originated in Great

Britain in the mid-1840s; known as dribblers because of the water or vapor trail deposited by their steam cylinders. Early British makers included H.J. Wood, Steven's Model Dockyards, Stevens Model Dockyards, Clyde Model Dockyard. German and U.S. makers also made steamers.

Steam railroad
A term still used by regulating bodies to separate ordinary railroads from electric railways, such as interurban and streetcar companies.

Storkleg
A locomotive with two small (in front) plus two large (in back) driving wheels, said to resemble a stork standing on one leg, though a stretch of one's imagination.

Switch
As a noun, a track unit with movable rails to divert rolling stock from one track to another; a.k.a. turnout. As a verb: to sort cars by destination on more than one track; a.k.a. classify, drill, or marshall.

Switchback
Track arrangement, often comprising two switches, that require a change of direction, usually to ascend a steep grade.

Talgo truck
Couplers joined to the truck as a single unit; when truck rotated on its axis, it carried coupler along with it. This combo helped keep a constant height for the coupler which helped it operate more smoothly.

Tank locomotive
A locomotive that is self contained with its own water and coal supplies located on its own frame rather than behind it in a tender.

Teakettle
A reference to any old locomotive, especially a leaky one.

Tender
The car that trails the loco and, as the name implies, tends to the loco's needs by providing fuel such as

wood, coil, or oil to fire the boiler; also supplies water needed for creating steam.

Tinplate
One of the earliest, most versatile toy train materials, harking back to the 1850s. Large sheets of tinned iron or steel were cut, rolled, or folded and assembled, then enameled, japanned, embossed, and later lithographed. Chief disadvantage is that tin toys and trains are subject to scratching and chipping when subjected to aggressive child's play.

Torpedo
Refers to the shape of popular streamlined locomotives from the 1930s such as the Lionel Burlington *City of Denver* and the Union Pacific *City of Portland*.

Toy railroads
Trademark term originated by Ives in 1907 to promote the concept of not just a train set, but an entire system of rolling stock, railside equipment, terminals. Similar concept was advanced by Märklin in Europe.

Toy train
Intended primarily for child's play and shunned by modelers; mass-produced in sizable numbers and more apt to be fanciful than realistic.

Truck
The entire wheel assembly on a locomotive and cars that includes a frame, springs to cushion the ride, one or more axles, a series of wheels affixed to axles, and bolsters that attach to frame. The axle-wheel combination is called a wheelset.

Turnout
American term for diverging track. British refer to it as a point.

Unit
A single machine, most often a diesel-electric typified by one frame and a coupler at each end; smallest indivisible portion of a loco which comprises one or more units coupled together by the engineer.

Unit train

A train transporting a single bulk cargo, usually grain or coal, from one shipper to one consignee without switching or classification en route.

Varnish

A slang term for a passenger car or entire train set, derived from the finish applied to wooden passenger cars.

Well Tank

A type of locomotive which carries its own water on its underside.

Wheelset

Term for axle-wheel combo.

Whyte system

Numerical method of describing wheel configuration; e.g., 4-6-2.

Wildcat

A runaway locomotive.

Wye

Arrangement of tracks forming letter "Y" used for turning locos and cars.

Zinkpest

German for "zinc plague." Certain train sets made of zinc-cast alloys resulted in terminal cases of metal fatigue that created warpage, cracking, and finally, being reduced to rubble. This affliction befell, most notably, the Dorfan sets from the 1930s; also some of Märklin's most desirable models, including the streamlined SK800 4-6-4 steam locomotive from 1940.

Leading Flags and Other Railway Acronyms

In railroad jargon, "flag" refers to real-life railroad lines of the past 200 years. Many of the flags' prototype (complete trains) liveries and logos live on in miniature as replicated by toy train makers. Many of these abbreviations now refer to obsolete or defunct lines, called fallen flags which exist today only as fond memories of a glorious past, often celebrated in song, cinema, folk lore, and literature. The insignias of these legendary railways are known as heralds. John McPhee in an Oct. 10, 2005, *New Yorker* article, "Coal Trains II," laments the passing of all four railroad properties represented in the popular game Monopoly—the Reading, Pennsylvania, Short Line, and B&O RR's—all sound investments when using Monopoly money, but fallen flags in the real world.

NORTH AMERICA

AA—Ann Arbor Railroad

ACL—Atlantic coast line

AND—Ashley, Drew & Northern

AL—Algoma Central (Wisconsin)

ALKA—Alaska Railroad

AM—Amtrak

AP—Atlantic & Union Pacific

ASA—Atlantic & St. Andrews

AT&SF—Atchison Topeka and Santa Fe (one of many railways celebrated in song)

AWP—Atlanta & West Point Railroad

B&A—Bangor & Aroostock

B&LE—Bessemer & Lake Erie

B&M—Boston & Maine Railroad

B&O—Baltimore & Ohio. One of nation's oldest lines, founded in 1830 and the first steam powered railroad in the U.S.

BN—Burlington Northern

C&NW—Chicago & Northwestern

C&O—Chesapeake & Ohio (known as the "Chessy")

CP—Central Pacific. Rival to the Union Pacific which linked with that railway to form the transcontinental railroad in 1869.

C&P—Clarendon & Pittsford

C&S—Colorado & Southern

CANP—Canadian Pacific (Canadian)

CB—Cotton Belt

CBQ—Chicago, Burlington, Quincy (Burlington Route)

CH—Chattanooga Traction

CAN—Canadian National (Canada)

CNJ—Central Railroad of New Jersey (Jersey Central Lines)

CNW—Chicago & Northwestern

COB—Chicago Outer Belt

CON—Conrail (became a fallen flag in 1999)

CPR—Canadian Pacifica Railways (Canadian)

CR—Clinchfield Railroad

CRI&P—Chicago, Rock Island & Pacific

D&H—Delaware & Hudson Railroad Corp.

DLW—Delaware, Lackawanna & Western

DSSA—Duluth, South Shore & Atlantic

DTI—Detroit, Toledo & Ironton

EL—Erie & Lackawanna

ERIE—Erie Railroad

FEC—Florida East coast

FGEX—Fruit Growers Express

FR—Frisco (St. Louis & San Francisco)

G&W—Genessee & Wyoming

GAEX—General American Express

GMO—Gulf Mobile & Ohio

GN—Great Northern

GTW—Grand Trunk Western Railway System

IC—Illinois Central Railroad. Another fallen flag, now part of Canadian National

IT—Illinois Terminal Railroad

KSC—Kansas City Southern

L&SJ—Laprarie & St. John. Canada's first rail service, begins in Quebec in 1836

L&N—Louisville & Nashville

LNA—Lewisville, New Albany & Corydon

LNE—Lehigh & New England

LV—Lehigh Valley

M&P—Maryland & Pennsylvnia

MC—Maine Central

MILW—Milwaukee Road (Chicago, Milwaukee, St. Paul & Pacific)

MKT—Missouri-Kansas-Texas Railroad Co. (known as the Katy)

MP—Missouri Pacific Railroad

MSL—Minneapolis & St. Louis

MTW—Marinette, Tomahawk & Western

N&W—Norfolk & Western Railroad

NH—New Haven (New York, New Haven & Hartford Railroad)

NKP—New York, Chicago & St. Louis (known as the Nickel Plate)

NVA—Nashville & Eastern Railroad

MP—Northern Pacific

NYC—New York Central System

ON—Oregon & Northwestern

ONNO—Ontario Northland (Canada)

OPE—Oregon, Pacific & Eastern

PAEL—Pacific Electric

PC—Penn Central

PE—Pittsburg & Lake Erie

PEAB—Peabody Short line

PFE—Pacific Fruit Express

PHD—Port Huron & Detroit

PRR—Pennsylvania Railroad

PSR—Petaluma & Santa Rosa Railroad

RDG—Reading Railroad

RFP—Richmond Fredericksburg & Potomac

RI—Rock Island (Chicago, Rock Island & Pacific). Celebrated in a Leadbelly folk classic.

RIO—Grande (Denver & Rio Grande Western Railroad)

RUT—Rutland Railroad (Vermont)

RV—Rahway Valley Railroad (New Jersey)

SAL—Seaboard Air Line (Florida coast)

SCL—Seaboard Coast Lines

SDRX—Sinclair

SIR—Sierra Railroad

SOO—Minneapolis, St. Paul & Sault Ste. Marie (known as SOO Line)

SOU—Southern Railway. An SOU terminal station that opened in 1909 in Chattanooga, Tenn., is immortalized in a Tex Beneke hit, "Chatanooga Choo Choo," and a museum so-named is a major tourist attraction.

SP—Southern Pacific (consumed by Union Pacific in 1996; recently merged with Santa Fe RR)

SPI—Spokane International Railway

SPS—Spokane, Portland & Seattle

SR—Southern Railway System

SRN—Sabine River & Northern

SSW—St. Louis, Southwestern

SUS—Susquehanna

T&P—Texas & Pacific (also designated as TEXP)

THB—Toronto, Hamilton & Buffalo (Canada)

TPW—Toledo, Peoria & Western (known as the Rocket)

UP—Union Pacific (now a conglomerate of 8 to 10 railroads)

USRA—Unites States Railroad Administration

UTLX—Union Tank Leasing Co.

VMC—Vermont Central

VR—Virginia Railway

VT—Virginia & Truckee Railway

W&A—Western & Atlantic

WAB—Wabash Railroad. Song "The Wabash Cannonball" was popularized by St. Louis sportscaster Dizzy Dean.

WM—Western Maryland Railway

WP—Western Pacific

OVERSEAS
Austria
OBB—Osterreichische Bundesbahnen (Austrian Federal Railways)

STLB—Steirmarkische Landesbahnen (Steirmark Provincial Railways)

Belgium

NMBS—Nationale Maatschapij van Belgische Spoorwegen (Belgian National Railways)

Czechoslovakia

CSD—Czechoslovakian State Railways

Denmark

DSB—Danske Statsbaner (Danish State Railways)

Great Britain

BR—British Railways (British National Railway). State-owned since 1948, replacing individual lines.

CLU—Central London Underground Railway

GE—Great Eastern

GN—Great Northern

LMS—London Midland and Scottish Railway. Incorporated into British Railways in 1948.

L&N—London & Northeastern

L&SW—London & Southwest

MLD—Midland Railway

SIR—Surrey Iron Railway. Started service in 1801 as the first commercial freight line.

France
CIT—Comite International des Transports par Chemins de Fer (International Committee for Railroad Transport)

ETAT—Chemins de fer d'Etat Francais (formerly French State Railways). Succeeded by SNCF; see below.

MD—Midi Railway

PLM—Paris-Lyon Mediterranee

PO—Paris-Orleans

SEA—St. Etienne-Andruezieux Railway. France's first steam-powered railway service, began in 1832.

SNCF—Société Nationale des Chemins de fer Français (private French railways were nationalized in 1938 under this heading)

Germany
DB—Deutsche-Bundesbahn Lines in West Germany adopted this designation in the late 1940s.

DR—The DRG designation no long applied during World War II, but the East German government retained the DR for Deutsche Reichsbahn.

DRG—Deutsche Reichsbahn railway system founded in the 1920s, operated under that name until 1945.

NF—Nuremburg-Furth, initiated the first German steam-powered rail service in 1835

Italy
FS—Ferrovie dello Stato (State Railways, Italy)

Luxemburg
CFL—Société Nationale Luxembourgeois (Luxemburg's national railway)

Netherlands
NS—Netherlandse Spoorwegen (Netherlands Railways). Dutch national railways.

Norway
NSB—Norges Statsbaner (Norway State Railway)

Spain
RENFE—Red Nacional de los Ferrocarriles Espanoles (National Network of Spanish Railways)

Transfesa—Transportes Ferroviarias Especiales S.A. (Specialized Rail Transport Association)

Sweden
SJ—Statens Jarnvagar (Swedish State Railways)

Switzerland
CFF—Chemins de fer Federaux (Swiss national railways—as opposed to private Swiss railway companies)

SBB—Schweizerische Bundesbahnen (Swiss Federal Railways)

Bibliography

Alexander, E., The *Collectors Book of the Locomotive,* Clarkson N. Potter, NY, 1966.

Bagdade, Susan and Al, *Collector's Guide to American Toy Trains,* Wallace Homestead Book Co., Radnor, PA.

Baker, Stanley L. and Virginia Brainard Kunz, *The Collector's Book of Railroadiana,* Hawthorn Books, 1976.

Carlson, Pierce, *Toy Trains: A History,* Justin Knowles Pub., Exeter, Devon, England, 1986

Carp, Roger, *The Art of Lionel Trains and American Dreams,* Kalmbach Pub., Waukesha Wis.

Glaab, John, The *Brown Book of Brass Locomotives,* 3rd. edition.

Godin, Serge Coluzzi, Count Antonio Giansanti Collection, The Trains on Avenue de Rumine, Crown

Pub., NY, 1984 (First published by New Cavendish Book/Editions, 1982.)

Fernandez, Don, *Trains: Railroading for Grown-up Boys (The Encyclyopedia of Collectibles, Vol. 15)*, Time-Life Books, NY, 1980.

Greenberg, Bruce C., *Legendary Lionel Trains*, Greenberg Pub., 7543 Main St., Sykesville, MD 21784 (one of the latest Greenberg's guides, which number over 20, devoted to major train makers—Lionel, Märklin, American Flyer, Ives, Marx).

Hertz, Louis, *Collecting Model Trains*, Mark Haber, Wethersfield, CT, 1956.

—, *New Roads to Adventure in Model Railroading*, Simmons-Boardman, 1952.

—, *Messrs. Ives of Bridgeport*, Mark Haber, 1950.

—, *Riding the Tinplate Rails*, Model Craftsman, 1944.

Hollander, Ron, *All Aboard!: The Story of Joshua Lionel Cowen and His Lionel Train Company*, Workman, NY, 1981.

Kimball, Ward, *Toys: Delights From the Past*, Applied Arts Publisher, 1978.

Klamkin, Charles, *Railroadiana: The Collector's Guide*, Funk & Wagnalls, 1976.

Levy, Allen, *A Century of Model Trains*, New Cavendish Books, 1986 (reprint of 1947 edition).

Peters, Dave Sr., *Railroadiana: Remembering the Iron Horse (Encyclopedia of Collectibles, Vol. 14)*, Time-Life, Alexandria, VA, 1980.

Ralston, Rick, *Cast-Iron Floor Trains*, www.ralstonantiques.com.

Reder, Gustav, Clockwork, *Steam and Electric: A History of Model Railways*, trans. by C. Hamilton Ellis, Ian Allan Pub., Shepperton, England, 1972.

Williams, Guy R., *The World of Model Trains*, Andre Deutsch, London, 1970.

Train Railways and Museums

There are nearly 500 operating historic railroads and railroad museums acoss the U.S. and Canada. This is merely a random sample.

Museum of Alaska Transportation and Industry
3800 West Neuser Drive, off Mile 47, Parks Highway
Wasilla, AK 99687
Web site: www.museumofalaska.org

California State Railroad Association
Corner of 2nd & I Streets, Old Sacramento
Sacramento, CA 95813
Web site: www.csrmf.org.

Canadian Museum of Rail Travel
1 Van Horn Street
Cranbrook, British Columbia, VIC 4H9
Web site: www.cyberlink.bc.ca/camal

Casey Jones Museum
(located less than a mile from crash site
where Jones was killed)

10901 Vaughan Road No. 1
Vaughan, MS 39179

Colorado Railroad Museum
17155 West 44th Avenue
Golden, CO 80402
Web site: www.crrm.org

Grand Canyon Railway
(Train Rides & Museum)
235 North Grand Canyon Boulevard
Williams, AZ
Web site: www.thetrain.com

Harmar Station
Museum and Operating Layout
220 Gilman Street
Harmar Village
Marietta, OH 45750
Web site: www.eekman.com/harmarstation/

Kennesaw Civil War Museum
2829 Cherokee Street
Kennesaw, GA 30144
Web site: www.ngeorgia.com/histgory/kcwn.html

Knott's Berry Farm Ghost Town & Calico Railway
80239 Beach Boulevard
Buena Partk, CA 90620
Web site: www.knotts.com

Missouri Museum of Transportation
3015 Barrett Station Road
St. Louis, MO 63122

Museum of Science and Industry
57th Street & Lake Shore Drive
Chicago, IL 60637
Web site: www.msichicagao.org

National Railroad Museum
2285 S. Broadway
Green Bay, WI 54304
Web site: *www.nationalmuseum.org.*

National Toy Train Museum
(One of the world's finest collections of toy trains)

300 Paradise Lane
Strasburg, PA 17579
Web site: www.traincollectors.org

New York Museum of Transportation
6393 East River Road
West Henrietta, NY 14586
Web site: www.rochester.ny.us/railmuseum.html

Redwood Valley Railway Corp.
2950 Magnolia, St.
Berkeley, CA 94705
Web site: members.aol.com/rvry/index.html

San Diego Model Railroad Museum
Balboa Park
1649 El Prado
San Diego, CA 92101
E-mail: SDModRailM@aol.com

Smithsonian Institution
Nation Museum of American History
14 Street and Constitution Ave.
Washington, D.C. 20560

Toy Train Depot
1991 North White Sands Blvd.
Alamogordo, NM 88310
Web site: www.quick.comt/toy

Train and Toy Collecting Organizations

A number of collecting organizations listed below may lack a permanent headquarters address. The mailing address could vary from time to time. Check current toy train periodicals to stay posted on such changes.

American Flyer Collectors Club (AFCC)
P.O. Box 13269
Pittsburgh, PA 15243

Ammonoosuc Vallery Railroad Associates
P.O. Box 48
Bath, NH 03740

Antique Toy Collectors Association
Rte 2, Box 5A
Baltimore, MD 21120

Canadian Railroad Historical Association
120 Rue St. Pierre
St. Constant, PQ
Canada J5A 2G9
(15 divisions across Canada)

Electric Railroaders Association
P.O. Box 3223, Grand Central Station
New York, NY 10163

Hornby Railway Collectors Association
2 Ravensmore Road
Sherwood, Nottingham NG5 2AH,
United Kingdom

Ives Train Society
P.O. Box 59
6714 Madison Road
Thompson, OH 44086
Website: members.aol.com/ivesboy/index.html

Key, Lock & Lantern
Website: www.klnl.org
(Railroadiana hardware)

Lehmann Gros Bahn (LGB) Model Railroad Club
1854 Erin Drive
Altoona, PA 16602-7612
Website: www.lgb.com/lgb_mrrclub.html
(2,000 members, mostly collectors)

Lionel Collectors Club of America (LCCA)
P.O. Box 479
La Salle, IL 61301

Lionel Operating Train Society (LOTS)
P.O. Box 66240
Cincinnati, OH 45247-5704

Lionel Railroader Club
26570 Twenty-three Mile Road
Chesterfield, MI 48051-1956

Märklin Enthusiasts of America
P.O. Box 189
Beverly, NJ 08010

Märklin Club of North America
P.O. Box 51559
New Berlin, WI 53151

National Association of S-Gaugers
280 Gordon Road
Matawan, NJ 07747

National Association of Timetable Collectors, Inc.
Norbert Shacklette
American Inn Road
Villa Ridge, MO 63089
Issues *Timetable Collector* newsletter and holds
annual convention

National Model Railroad Association (NMRA)
4121 Cromwell Road
Chattanooga, TN 37421

National Railway Historical Society
P.O. Box 58547-D
Philadelphia, PA 19102-8547
E-mail: nrhs@compuserve.com

O Scale Kings
560 East Church Street
Lewisville, TX 75057
E-mail: prbrass@flash.net

Toy Train Collectors Society (TTCS)
109 Howedale Drive
Rochester, NY 14616-1534

Toy Train Operating Society (TTOS)
P.O. Box 248
Strasburg, PA 17579

Train Collectors Association (TCA)
P.O. Box 248
Stroudsburg, PA 18360
(717) 687-8623

Virginia Train Collectors, Inc.
P.O. Box 7114
Richmond, VA 23221

Toy and Model Train Auctioneers

Noel Barrett Auctions
P.O. Box 300
Carversville, PA 18913
Web site: www.noelbarrett.com

Bertoia Auctions
2141 DeMarco Drive
Vineland, NJ 08360
Web site: www.BertoiaAuctions.com

Butterfield & Butterfield
1244 Sutter Street
San Francisco, CA 94109
Web site: Butterfield.com

Christie's East
219 East 67th Street
New York, NY 10041

Continental Auctions
447 Stratford Road
P.O. Box 193
Sheboygan, WI 53081

Garth's Auctions
2690 Stratford Road
Delaware, OH 43015

Leslie Hindman Auctioneers
122 North Aberdeen Street
Chicago, IL 60607
Web site: www.lesliehindman.com

Randy Inman Auctions
P.O. Box 726
Waterville,ME 04903-0726
Web site: www.InmanAuctions.com

James Julia, Inc.
P.O. Box 830
Fairfield, ME 04937
Web site: www.juliaauctions.com

Mapes Auctioneers & Appraisers
Vestal Parkway West
Vestal, NY 13850

Ted Maurer Auctions
1931 North Charlotte Street
Pottstown, PA 19464
Web site: www.maurerail.com

Morphy Auctions
2000 North Reading Road
Denver, PA 17517
E-mail: Morphy@morphyauctions.com

New England Toy Train Exchange
110-112 Beaver Brook Road, Unit 2
Danbury, CT 06811
Web site: www.newenglandtoytrainexchange.com

Richard Opfer Auctioneering, Inc.
1919 Greenspring Drive
Timonium, MD 21093
Web site: www.opferauction.com

Lloyd Ralston Toys
549 Howe Avenue
Shelton, CT 06484
Web site: www.lloydralstontoys.com

RM Auctions
One Classic Car Drive
Blenheim, Ontario
Web site: www.rmauctions.com

RSL Auctions
P.O. Box 1752
Bridgehampton, NY 11932
E-mail: raytoys@aol.com

Skinner Auctions, Inc.
357 Main Street
Bolton, MA 01740
Web site: www.skinnerinc.com

Sotheby's
1334 York Avenue at 72nd Street
New York, NY 10021

Stout Auctions
529 SR 28 East
Williamsport, IN 47993
Web site: www.stoutauctions.com

Phillip Weiss Auctions, Inc.
1 Neal Court
Oceanside, NY 11572
Web site: www.philipweissauctions.com

Overseas Auction Houses

Auction Team Köln
P.O. Box 50
Köln, Germany 50968
E-mail: Auction@Brecker.com

Brooks
81 Westside
London, SWA 9AY,
Great Britain
0171-288-8000

Christie's
South Kensington
85 Old Brompton Road
London SW7 3LD

Galerie Andre
Place de Londres 13
B 1050 Bruxelles, Belgium

Hanseatisches Auktionshaus für Historica
Husken/Shafer OHG
Neur Wall 75-2000 Hamburg 36
Germany 40/36137-38
Web site: www.hanseatiches-auktionshaus.de

Phillips Blenstock House
7 Bleinheim Street, New Bond Street
London, England
WIY Oas
1-629-6602

Vectis Auctions Ltd.
Thornaby Stockton on Tees
TS17 9Jz, England
Web site: www.vectis.co.uk

Weinheimer Auktionshaus
Rolf Richter
Karlsruher Strasse 2/8
D 6940 Wenheim
Germany 06201/15997
Web site: www.weinheimer-auktionshaus.de

Toy and Model Rail Road Shows and Meets

In additional to national events, countless local and regional train shows and meets are held throughout the year. Consult such publications as *Classic Toy Trains, Antique Toy World, Antiques & the Arts Weekly, Model Railroader,* or your local newspapers for show dates and times.

Greenberg's Train & Hobby Show
P.O. Box 1192
Lombard, IL 60148
Web site: www.greenbergshows.com

Lionel Collectors Club of America
International Convention
Information: Ray F. Long
University of South Carolina Coliseum
3702 Greenbriar Drive
Columbia, SC 29206
(803) 782-1087

Morphy's Toy, Doll & Adv. Show
York Fairgrounds Expo Center
York, PA
E-mail: *danmorphy@dejazzd.com*
(Held in Oct. & Feb.)

St. Vincent DePaul's Model Train & Toy Show
1510 DePaul Street
Elmont, Long Island, NY 11003
(Held in October)

Train Collectors of America (TCA)
Semiannual Shows: April & October
P.O. Box 248
Strasburg, PA 17579

Westchester Toy & Train Assoc.
P.O. Box 149
Route 100 & Terrytown Road
Spencertown, NY 12165

Train Collecting Publications

Classic Toy Trains
Kalmbach Pub. Co.
P.O. Box 1612
Waukesha, WI 53187
Web site: Classictoytrains.com

Garden Railways
Kalmbach Pub. Co.
P.O. Box 1612
Waukesha, WI 53187
(Outdoor model railroading)

Mainline Modeler
Hundman Publishing
5115 Monticello Drive
Edmonds, WA 98020
(206) 743-2607

N Scale Collector
(newsletter)
3535 Stine Road, #108
Bakersfield, CA 93309-6610

48/ft O-Scale News
Box 51
Elmhurst, IL 60126

O Gauge Railroading
33 Sheridan Road
Poland, OH 444514
Web site: www.ogaugerr.com

S-Gaugian
Heimburger Pub. Co.
7236 West Madison Ave.
Forest Park, IL 60130-1765

The Dispatch
(Model S-gauge newsletter)
220 Swedesboro Road
Gibbstown, NJ 08027-1504

Railfan & Railroad
108 Phil Hardin Road
P.O. Box 700
Newton, NJ 07860-0700
E-mail: carstens@carstens-publications.com

Railroad Model Craftsman
Carsten Publications
P.O. Box 700
Newton, NJ 07860-0700
E-mail: carstens@carstens-publications.com
Includes *Toy Trains* combined with *Electric Trains and Hobby Railroading, Model & Railway News*

The O-Gauger & The Model Maker
Railway Museum Quarterly
P.O. Box 370
Tujunga, CA 91043-0370

Train Collectors Quarterly
P.O. Box 248
Strasburg, PA 17579
E-mail: Toytrain@traincollectors.org

Trains Magazine
Kalmbach Pub. Co.
P.O. Box 1612
Waukesha, WI
53187-1612
Web site: www.trains.com

Publications devoted to railway museums:

Empire State Railway Museum Annual
Kalmbach Pub. Co.
P.O. Box 1612
Waukesha, WI 53187

Lionel Train & Seashell Museum
Sarasota, FL 33580

Railway Museum Quarterly
Association of Railway Museums, Inc.
P.O. Box 370
Tujunga, CA 91043

Repair and Restoration Services

Russ & Sheila Harrington
1805 Wilson Point Road
Baltimore, MD 21220
E-mail: Russsheila@comcast.net

Pat Neil
109 Medallion Center
Dallas, TX 75214
Web site: www.trinsandtoys.com

Joe Mania
Downtown Trains
17 Douglas Road
Freehold, NJ 00728

Sy Shreckinger
P.O. Box 104
East Rockaway, NY 11518

Tin Toy Works
Joe Freeman
1313 North 15th Street
Allentown, PA 18102
E-mail: Tintoyworks@enter.net

Bill White
Vintage Lionel Train Exchange
1600 Smith Street 4230
Houston, TX 77002

ACKNOWLEDGMENTS

We wish to thank the following individuals and organizations for their input and permission to use images and quotations. Noel Barrett Auctions, Bertoia Auctions, Ted Maurer Auctions, Morphy Auctions, Lloyd Ralston Auctions, James Julia Auctions, Catherine Saunders Watson of Antique Week, and Madaline and Josh Friz for computer and photographic assistance beyond the call of duty.

INDEX

Page numbers in *italics* refer to illustrations